Kick Ass Your Life

Kick Ass Your Life

Get Clear, Get Moving, Get the Life you Deserve

by
Ann Hobbs

A catalogue record for this book is available from the British Library. ISBN: 978-0-9934652-0-8

Contents

Acknowledgements

A big thank you to my family for being my rock, supporting me throughout my journey - my husband Nigel and my three beautiful children, Chris, Nick and Harry. Also to my Mum, Dad and sisters, all so terribly affected by the tragic loss of Susan – she left a big hole in all our lives.

To the acupuncturist who lifted a huge weight off my shoulders when he said "I see this all the time," helping me realise that I wasn't going mad after all!

A big shout out to all my clients for teaching me so much along the way - this book would not have become a reality had they not had the courage to ask for help and been willing to change. It has been a pleasure to work with you all.

To Sandy Draper for helping me get my book out into the world in the best possible shape and to Paul Walkinshaw for supporting the book.

And finally, love and gratitude to my sister Susan, who left us in tragic circumstances 15 years ago.

Dear Susan,

I am writing this letter to you because I want you to know about the journey I have taken since you left this earth. I think of you every day and know that when I am working and healing my clients you are with me. Thank you for the beautiful dance we had not so long ago, when I felt completely at peace and enjoyed the moment. Even though I can no longer physically see you, I sense your beautiful soul is still near me.

Since losing you, my journey has been a difficult one, but one I wouldn't have gone on if you hadn't been taken from me. I felt lost, alone and frightened, but I want to thank you for being my catalyst for change – although I would rather you be here now laughing and joking with me.

I am trying to do good in the world by helping people to heal their lives, so that they, like me, can end their struggle and find joy and bliss and fully understand who they are. Over the years, I have often felt guilty that I wouldn't be doing this work if you were still here. I have now accepted this and realise that this is your legacy to me: to help others when they are feeling lost and confused, as I once was.

I hope, wherever you are now, that you are happy. You are the inspiration for my work. I couldn't have done it, if you hadn't been in my life.

Love Ann xx

Introduction

Creating Longer-lasting Change

WARNING!

- This book doesn't promise to change your life in 90 days.

- This is not the last self-help book you will ever read.

- This book is not a 'quick fix'.

I believe that change is a journey, and to really affect change in your life permanently takes a lifestyle choice.

Change isn't just for Christmas – it's for life!

You've picked up this book for a reason. You are seeking answers. That is how I felt when I felt lost and didn't know where to start. All I knew was that I felt lost, and so I started on a journey of personal understanding and self-development to find the answers.

If this sounds familiar then read on.

Perhaps you don't know what the problem is but you do know that you have all these feelings of being lost, and maybe also feel anxious or scared and don't know how to move forwards or even where to start.

There comes a point in all our lives when we feel like this. Sometimes an event happens that we simply can't cope with, such as losing a family member or a relationship break-up or ill health. All of these, and a whole host of other happenings, can be a catalyst for change, and make you feel as though you are hitting a brick wall and don't know where to start. You may also be feeling:

- **lonely**

- **afraid**

- **angry**

- **frustrated**

- **depressed**

- **tired**

- **like something needs to change**

- **there is more to life**

When we feel lost, we feel like we are not in control: everything is happening around us and we can't seem to get off the hamster wheel. We keep going round and round, doing the same old thing time and time again. While all the time knowing, that if we keep doing the same thing, we will end up in the same mess again.

Or perhaps you are having these feelings in your life right now because you need to take a different path; you need new information and a different awareness. So in fact you are not lost at all, and this is your wake-up call.

Are you ready to listen? Are you ready to change?

You are not alone. I see many people in my practice who are in this situation and it is easy to change when you follow the steps described in the following chapters.

When I was lost, I felt as though I was the only person on the planet with problems and so I couldn't talk about them. But, in fact, when I started talking to other people about it, people understood and I found that at some point in their lives they had felt the same way too. What a relief to know I was not alone.

> *Feeling lost is a myth.*
> *You may feel lost but you are not lost.*

When I have felt lost, I have usually been at a crossroads in my life. It has been a time to reflect, to make new decisions, or perhaps walk away from things that were not working. So I wasn't really feeling lost at all; it was just a time for change. Our minds don't like change at all because it creates this feeling of being unstable and insecure. But, if you think about it, everything is changing every second of our lives. We, and the world we live in, are in a constant state of change but still we see change as something scary, an event to be feared, that we can't possibly cope with and it will all be doom and gloom.

I know how it feels to be lost; when your world feels like it's falling around your ears. You just need the strength and courage to stand up to it all and find a different path, a more fulfilling one, and find the answers that you are seeking.

Catalyst for change

On 24th November, 1999, when I was eight and half months pregnant, my sister aged 35 was brutally murdered in her own home. From that moment, my whole life changed. My family crumbled at the news, as we each tried to deal with our grief in our own way. I was thrown into a mist of unknown feelings. How was I supposed to deal with something like that? I felt lost, lonely and afraid.

The following days and months seemed to go by in a blur. We were thrust into the world of police procedure and having to deal with many things that had never entered our lives before. My sister had become a celebrity! Her pictures were all over the local and national newspapers and throughout the local area, as the police searched for her killer. It felt as though the colour had drained out of my world, I felt very unsafe and lost. But life had to continue. I still had to take the kids to school and my life seemed normal still.

In the midst of this whirlwind, I gave birth to my third son, Harry. I just thought of the saying, 'When one dies another is born', but I didn't expect it to happen within one family.

Later we had to endure a long Crown Court trial, 150 miles away from home, and this was when I first noticed my feelings of fear and anxiety. Every day it was a struggle to get up in the morning. I had panic attacks and thought I was going to die. The world became very unsafe and I trusted no one. Afterwards, life seemed to go down a slippery slope but I didn't notice it. Instead, I papered over my emotions, went back to work and carried on. Then I hit a brick wall.

It started by not wanting to go out of the house alone, for example, to go food shopping. I felt dizzy all the time, nauseous and slept a lot. I didn't know what was happening to me and felt very frightened. My thoughts turned to my sister and the birth of my son. Was that the problem? *Why couldn't I cope?* I felt like a failure so I retreated into myself. (In fact, I now know that this is very common in depression – it is just too much to bear and often the response is to simply disconnect from life.)

With hindsight it seems obvious, these were massive events in my life but I couldn't see it. After all, who wouldn't be affected by them? And it's something I have seen many times since becoming a therapist. Clients often don't realise how big the events that have happened in their lives are and try to carry on as normal. When the grief or pain or issue becomes too hard to bear, many people respond by trying, as I did, to block out their thoughts and feelings because they feel ashamed and not good or strong enough. When forced to examine my feelings closer, I found my catalyst for change. This was my wake-up call.

I felt strongly that something had to change. I could no longer live like this and decided to do something different. Of course, I went down the usual route of seeing the doctor first, but I felt there was something more. I wanted answers that the doctor with his prescription pad couldn't give.

Somehow I found the courage to follow a different path. I knew if I wanted answers to 'why', so that I could understand and be in control of my life, then I needed a different set of rules.

The first time we ask for help is always the hardest but when I finally plucked up courage to tell my acupuncturist how I was feeling he said to me, 'I see this all the time.' It felt as though a huge weight had been lifted off my shoulders and I wondered why I had left it so long to ask for help.

I decided to WAKE UP to my life, which led me on a journey into holistic therapies. I began training as an aromatherapist and reflexologist, and this helped me understand what was happening to my mind and body, and make changes in my life that were needed. I read many self-help books to find the one answer that I was really seeking. However, I came to the conclusion that there was no single answer that could fix it. There was no magic pill. I had to change the way I was living and thinking.

I began to see that my catalyst for change had been a truly life-changing event and I gave myself time to grieve. What I was going through was huge and I accepted it, not trying to push it away further. Foremost I forgave myself for not coping and learnt how to be kinder to myself – love myself no matter what. I became a teacher to others and this, in turn, helped me to realise my own negative patterns. In my work I was healing others and in turn they were healing me.

Over the 15 years that I have worked in the self-development world, I have met many people who have also been my greatest teachers. I have learnt a lot about myself, my insecurities and the beliefs and fears that were holding me back. It took time and courage to look deeply within, to begin my journey of self-discovery, but I knew I had to do it. So I put on my big girl pants, accepted where I was, took responsibility and instantly felt a little better.

It's hard for me to put my finger on the thing that changed my life because it was a combination of things that I've explored about myself over the years, that I have faced and I still continue to learn. My mission, however, is to teach you how to achieve what I did in a shorter space of time and that is what I want to share with you in this book.

But for starters, let me reassure you that you are not alone and, as a therapist, I continually see the same common problems again and again. They are as follows…

- We think we are broken and need *someone* to fix us.

- We continually put a plaster over the problem.

- We look at the wrong problem.

You are not broken

I see so many people using holistic therapies, coaching and so on to simply *fix* themselves, but this leads to the negative thought that *there is something wrong with you*, which is very overwhelming and doesn't help you know where to start. It is a myth.

> *You are not broken, so you don't need to fix anything at all.*

I also found that, whilst we often seem to deal with the issue, we don't get to the core problem. For example, one of my clients asked me if I could help her with her sleep issues. I said 'no' because I wanted to really understand *why* she couldn't sleep and get to the core of the problem. The real issue was that she didn't feel confident enough to go for the job she wanted. When we worked on that issue, her sleep was no longer the problem. If I had said 'yes' to working on her sleep problem, we would have been continually fixing the same thing; we would have simply put a plaster over the problem.

Now putting a plaster over an issue is easier, don't get me wrong, however, it will not only take longer, but you are likely to find yourself back in exactly the same place and not knowing how to get out of it. This will be a continual fixing process.

So if you feel as though you have *done* self-development work and used a number of different therapies (as I did) and it hasn't worked for you, or if you are starting out on your journey, then my Kick Ass programme will teach you the foundations that you need to experience longer-lasting change.

My philosophy is to teach you lifelong skills so that you can build a successful life. In my work I have found that many people really don't know what lies at the root of their feelings and just don't understand what their problem is. They may have found some success through one particular self-help therapy or another, but the effects don't last. That's because often we look at the wrong problem; we need to look at the very core of the problem.

Don't look at the presenting problem, dig deeper.

I can't promise you that you won't ever feel lost again – I know that I have been lost several times in my life – but I do know that if you follow the simple steps in this book then, whenever you do feel lost, you will know how to get out of it faster. You may think that you don't ever want to feel like this again but in reality you will. You can't run from these emotions and feelings because they will always need to be expressed in certain parts of your life.

This book is not about never getting lost or stuck again, it's about having the tools at your fingertips so you know how to get to the core of your problem quickly and then change it around.

Chapter 1

Tools of Positive Change

On a scale of 1–10, with 10 being amazing and 1 being rubbish, how are you feeling right now?

You may be feeling overwhelmed at this point, perhaps already thinking that you have a lot to 'fix' or sort out, but in fact you haven't. All you need to do is to keep reading and this book will guide you through the process of change step by step.

When we are lost, we often scrabble around and can't see the light at the end of the tunnel. We become stuck and can't seem to move on. It feels as though we are in a dark place and can't see the answers. I've felt like this many times in my life and this is where many of my clients describe being, but often all they need is a new perspective on things. You need to know where you are, how you got there and where you want to go.

This book will give you the information that you need in order to affect change; it will put you on the right path so that you can live the life you want rather than the one you don't.

It's a lifestyle change, not a quick fix.

What you'll need to create positive change:

- **A new set of rules and information.**

- **Awareness.**

- **To know where you are right now.**

- **To know what you want.**

- **To look at the core of the problem and not the presenting problem.**

We all feel strong emotions and don't know how to express them; and we all feel lost, insecure and frightened from time to time. Self-development is not about being happy and positive all of the time. It's about allowing yourself to feel and express your emotions. So when you are feeling down and sad it's OK to cry to release those feelings and when you are feeling frustrated express them in a safe way. Most people don't listen to, or even express, their emotions but it is important to do so because unexpressed emotions can cause dis-ease in our bodies. That is why a lot of my clients come to me with physical symptoms. I believe physical symptoms are the last to manifest and the first to go. Self-development is about knowing yourself well enough so that you feel safe to express these emotions and trust and listen to what you need.

What will you achieve by the end of this book?

You will have a greater sense of understanding about why you are feeling lost and how to move forwards from this point in time. You will understand the pitfalls of change and how not to succumb to them, so that you can affect change quickly and get to the core of your problem. I want you to be able to ask yourself that 'better question', so that you are armed with tools that you can use over and over again when life gets difficult, and understand what is at the core of the problem so you don't just plaster over the presenting issue.

Action is required

Most people don't take time to really reflect on what they want, so you are already one step ahead by reading this book and committing to doing the exercises. Action is a really big part of change and it speeds up the transformation. You don't have to commit long periods of time, it could be simply 10–30 minutes a day – and don't feel guilty about spending time on yourself just because it is something for you. Think of it as a necessity to live the life you want.

I encourage you to do the exercises because they will create a new pattern of thinking and help you move forwards. It is like building muscle, the more you lift weights (take action) then the stronger the muscle will become. If you don't take action then the process is likely to take longer and, of course, I want you to move out of that lost feeling quickly so that you can live an amazing life.

These are the exercises that I have used with clients over the years and they have achieved fantastic results.

What you will need

- A journal for the exercises.

- A music player on which to play your visualisations.

Journaling

I've been journaling for around three years and love it. Writing down your feelings and thoughts is really healing because it helps to get everything out of your head and on to paper. This may seem like a chore at first but regularly writing in your journal will create a habit and it will become easier the more you do it. So, I would advise that you set a regular time to journal, either in the morning or in the evening. Find somewhere quiet so that you can reflect. Write down your thoughts and feelings freely because:

- No one but you is meant to read it.

- It is good to go back and see how far you have come.

So don't freak out that you can't possibly put your words onto paper because someone else might see it. They won't. Your journal is your private space to be open and be yourself. Don't be frightened to express yourself; they are just feelings, words and thoughts. They have no power over you. Give yourself permission to express yourself in a safe place.

Questions

I love asking the right question and this book is filled with some thought-provoking ones. Journaling will help you keep track of where you are and what else you need to do. You will also have a space for your 'aha' moments so that you can reflect back. Sometimes we can't see how far we have come because we can't quite remember how we felt in the beginning. We change and then it feels as though we have always been that way. As soon as the pain goes away we tend to forget. So notice the little changes in yourself, notice the way you even smile or laugh more. This is progress. I will be checking back in with you at the end of the book so watch out!

Visualisations

The visualisations in this book have come to me whilst working with my clients and they have proved to be very effective. They can be done anytime you choose during the day and when you start using them you will find that they will help you to move forwards fast. I love to do my visualisations when I go to bed because it helps me to go to sleep in a positive mood. Again choose a regular quiet time, commit and stick to it.

Affirmations

An affirmation is just a positive statement but it can be a really helpful tool when you are trying to turn around negative beliefs about yourself. The right words, repeated often enough, can help bring positivity to any situation. So if you are thinking negative thoughts then you can replace them with an affirmation. Create your affirmations in the present tense (i.e. 'I am…') so they become part of your present experience, not something out there in the future.

One of the ways I keep myself on track is putting an affirmation on my phone as a reminder on the days that I need it, or writing it down on a card and putting in my diary or purse so that I can see it often. Get creative and find what works for you. I've included an affirmation at the end of each chapter to help you.

Let's start with the affirmation that I love to give my clients because the truth is you *are* amazing. Now, are you ready to kick ass your life?

Affirmation

'I am amazing.'

Chapter 2

Rules of Change

Before you start changing anything, there are three rules that can guide the process of transformation. There are also some pitfalls to avoid, so here follows some important guidelines that you may find helpful before you start changing anything.

You, the creator

Think for a moment about this concept:

We are the creators of our lives.

I believe we are the creators of our lives and most of our problems are what we have learnt. Therefore I have great news for you, you can simply unlearn them and create what you do want. But in order to change, we need a new set of rules.

1. **Know your why.**

2. **Make a decision to change.**

3. **Take responsibility – you are the creator of your life.**

Let's look at each rule in more detail.

Rule 1: Know your why

When things are going wrong in life and we have these feelings of being lost, we sometimes try to change external things. For example, we think it must be our job, our husband, our children, and if we change them then we will feel better.

Wrong!

In order to transform your life you don't need to change your job, leave your relationship or go on retreat to India for six months (although that would be great). All you need to do is be willing to change YOU, look at how you view the situation, how your story is contributing to your set of beliefs about the situation. I often find when clients change their perception it has a positive knock-on effect in their lives. By feeling more in control of something that you can change your confidence will increase, you will immediately start feeling good about yourself and this, in turn, increases your motivation to change. So when you start feeling good about yourself you will achieve your goal quicker. Believe me things can change in an instant when you get a new perspective on it.

Case Study

I first saw my client because she wanted to take a year's sabbatical from work. She said she wanted to 'go travelling'. This didn't resonate as being the real reason and so I told her it would probably be advisable to stop, don't change anything just yet. I asked her to be willing to explore what the real reason was. After some sessions with me she said that she wanted to take a sabbatical so that she could do the things she wanted, have time for her and enough time to do the things she wanted.

Now this was a true turning point. I felt that resonated with her and I felt it important that when people asked her why she was taking a sabbatical that she should say 'time for myself'. She thought that her employer would find it acceptable to have a sabbatical if she went travelling – isn't that why

everyone takes a sabbatical? When she established her
why, her employer offered her a year sabbatical (something
unheard of in her company) and it was easy to obtain.

So my client didn't change a thing at first, instead she explored what was at the root of her need for change. In fact, I tell all my clients not to change anything. Your job may be horrible but if you don't find the time to really explore who you are then you will, unwittingly, just go find the same job as you had before.

The very first step is to find your motivation – because it's not easy to change, it's not easy to break all the rules so you need to know 'YOUR WHY' – just like my client above.

My why

I was frustrated at the beginning because I didn't know how to change. I had to change for my family and myself, but I didn't know where to start. I don't want other people to feel like that; there is no need. You don't have to struggle with life; it can be joyous and fun, even while you are trying to find meaning and success in your life.

When I think about giving up, even when I was writing this book, I just think about other people struggling and know that if I didn't put myself out there, or my story, then I would be doing the world a disservice. I know how it feels and I don't want a living soul ever to be in the place I once was – lost, lonely, frustrated and anxious – there is ABSOLUTELY no need!

Change isn't easy, but it is more fulfilling. Don't take the easy
route! Get motivated and stay motivated!

WHAT IS YOUR WHY?

Take time to whip out your journal and write down the answers to the following questions. Answering them will help you to stay motivated when times are hard and you just want to give up, so keep this somewhere safe – perhaps at the very beginning of your journal – and read it again when you think of giving up or it feels too hard and you think you can't do it.

- Why are you reading this book?

- Why do you want to change?

- How do you want to feel?

When you feel like giving up then take the time to re-read your answers. Or write your answers on a big piece of paper and stick it up on a wall or on your desktop where you can see it every day. Now you have your motivation the second rule is about making a decision.

Rule 2: Make a decision to change

The second step is simply to make a decision. A decision to change! You are now armed with your 'why', so now you need to make a commitment to change.

This is your chance to actually be aware of what is going on, take responsibility and then take action to change. Some people don't listen to the warning signs, they just continue on with their lives. But if you ignore the warning signs they will get bigger and bigger until you listen. Let me invite you simply to be open to change right now and make a decision. You don't need all the answers to your questions; you just need to be willing to change and to trust that you will find a way.

Don't let other people affect this decision because you are not changing for them; this is for you, to make your life happier. So be careful that you are not changing for others, this is totally for you – although you may find more motivation by thinking about your children or family, and knowing that your change will have a positive impact on their lives too.

Even if you feel uncomfortable about opening up to the fact that you have these feelings, just have a willingness to look and continue with the exercises. You don't need to stand up in front of all your friends and family and say 'I have a problem', as you might in an AA session, you can keep it quiet for now – it's just between you and me!

The decision or willingness to change will come from a place of within; you don't need anyone else's permission to change. You just need to give yourself permission. That is all.

Make a decision to change, for you.

This is the moment where I hope you will say to yourself, 'Enough is enough. I can't do this anymore!' Don't forget I know how this feels so make a firm commitment to yourself that you want change and this will give you a solid foundation to start your process of transformation.

Do you feel like a failure?

Do you think you are the only one feeling this way?

You are not a failure. You are courageous.

How can I be sure?

Because not everybody takes this step – not everyone seeks help and actually puts their hand up to say, 'I'm feeling lost and I need help.' Perhaps because they think that seeking help is a sign of failure.

Let me tell you that it is not!

Being an empowerment coach and holistic therapist, I can tell you from experience that I see this all the time and it amazes me that everybody else thinks they are unique, they are the only ones feeling this way. Let's get something straight – right now – there are thousands of people out there feeling the way you are but either they are not ready to change or they are too scared to ask for help. Don't be one of them because you can change.

You are courageous.

To acknowledge that you are feeling lost and scared takes courage. Not everyone can admit to those feelings and so won't be reading this book, or be looking to make changes - because you do have to *own* up to those feelings, you have to acknowledge them and not paper over the cracks, as I did.

What do you need right now?

What you need right now is hope, answers and knowledge. You need to go down a different path because if you just do the same things you have done before, then you will end up at the same destination. All you need to change is new information. I will help you; I'm here to hold your hand.

HAVE YOU MADE YOUR DECISION?

So you need to make a decision now, before we move on. Whip out your journal, sit quietly and simply ask yourself the following questions.

- Do you want to change?

- Are you willing to take charge or your life and make a solid commitment to yourself?

- If the answer is yes, great, let's move on. You are ready.

If it is no, then still read on because you may find the answers to why you don't want to change and then you can come back to this question and have a more definitive answer.

Rule 3: Take responsibility – You are the creator of your life

You also need to take on the belief that you are the creator of your own life, even when it feels like you are not in control. Do you feel that life is happening to you? You are creating everything that is happening in your life through your thoughts, beliefs and actions. This is not to say that you are to 'blame' for where you are and how lost you feel. But we need to take responsibility for how we are responding to it. If we fail to take responsibility then we cannot transform it. It is all about taking control of your life. When you take control then you can transform your life.

> *If you don't take responsibility for your life you can't transform it.*

I became aware of this rule about taking responsibility when a client reiterated this point one day.

Case Study

One of my clients continuously came back to see me month after month and nothing was really changing. I felt like I had let her down and wasn't making her feel better. One session she was particularly bad and the first thing she said to me was 'Oh Ann, I knew I had to come and see you so that you could fix me.' I stepped back and questioned this and in my head said, 'No I won't, but I'll show you how you can help yourself.'

It was a pivotal moment for me as a therapist because I realised that I was unconsciously taking responsibility for her, that was why I was getting frustrated and she wasn't changing.

Often we don't take responsibility for what happens to us. Instead it seems easier to hand the reins over to our families, our therapist and our friends, which is a huge burden for them. What's more, if we don't take responsibility for our problems then we can't transform them. Giving the responsibility to someone else might fix the problem in the short term, but it will soon return with a vengeance demanding to be resolved again.

How do I know when I'm not taking responsibility?

You will simply be blaming your job, your husband, your kids or anything else but yourself. Everything else will be a priority. You will put yourself last and even try helping others, as it seems easier than helping yourself. This is quite normal and everyone does this from time to time so don't be too hard on yourself. So trust me when I say you are indeed creating everything that is happening right now.

This concept is sometimes quite hard to grasp and you might feel that certain events are beyond your control. I know that I wasn't responsible for my sister being killed, but it took me years to understand the fact that I was responsible for *how I was feeling about it*: the guilt I was experiencing and how my emotions were. I was responsible for getting myself out of that hole and no one was coming to save me. They would certainly help me but they weren't coming to save me, only I could do that. It might sound harsh, but you will feel in control when you accept that no one can take responsibility for you except YOU.

KICK ASS YOUR LIFE

Case Study

My client's mother physically abused her when she was a child. Now that shouldn't have happened to her, but in order to move past this pain my client had to learn how to take responsibility for the way she was feeling, the pain she was holding, for the simple reason of wanting to transform her life. This took a little while but when she realised that unless she took responsibility for her feelings then she would carry her pain for the rest of her life, she found the courage to take responsibility and transform it. It was a beautiful and tearful moment. She was able to move past this and resolve some of the issues she had with her mother. My client was able to continue her life free of this emotional pain. She felt lighter and happier to continue her journey.

> Responsibility is not the same as blame. Blame just makes you the victim and puts you in a negative place where you draw an invisibility cloak around yourself, so you can't see the next step. Each person needs to take responsibility for their own problems so that they can transform them.

If we change, the people around us change.

The thing that keeps me going through any kind of transformation – because change isn't easy – is the knowledge that when I change, the people around me change too, especially my children. I want my children to believe a different a set of rules, to believe they can do anything they want in life, so I need to be a shining example (which I'm not always!).

This amazes me when it happens but I've seen it happen in my life and in my clients' lives. For example, in the case study given above,

30

that particular client kept telling me how, as she transformed her life, her mother seemed happier too, and that she was now talking about different things in life – just simple things but nevertheless things that my client noticed.

This is the magic of change – you also change the lives of the people around you. If you are a shining example then others will be inspired too and join you on the journey.

On the other hand, you may also find that some people won't like you changing. It will wobble those people and make them feel insecure. Be compassionate towards them, and remember they have feelings too and may feel as though they have to get to know you all over again. So be gentle with yourself and with others around you because they will be feeling insecure and frightened too.

Why is change perceived as being hard?

No one, yes you heard correctly, no one likes change. It unsettles us and makes us feel vulnerable. When I see clients for the very first time, we talk about their problems and then when I say that I can help them the client invariably drops into fear. One time, a client actually clutched her chest and I thought I had upset her! But she simply said, 'What will I be like without my problems?' She felt fearful and didn't realise she could change.

I see this all the time and many people never manage to move past their fear of change, or even acknowledge the possibility that they can change. Some people don't even get started, so by simply reading this book you are one step closer. You may find that fear sometimes clutches you again and stops you in your tracks, and you start believing that you can't change. In reality you can. It is only the fear of the unknown making you falter.

At times like these, just remember that however much we plan our day, for instance, there are some things that we cannot plan for; things just happen. So, try to think of change from this perspective too because, even if you are accustomed to each day being more or less the same, we know there are never any certainties in life. Nothing ever stays the same. Things change all the time and it's just that we don't necessarily notice it.

Change is exciting, a little scary but exciting.

Turn your thinking around

If you look at it another way and start thinking that change is exciting then you get a different perspective on it. And if you are genuinely fearful of change then you might find it easier to take little steps each day to acclimatise to this new way of thinking (see the exercise below for more guidance). I don't say this to unsettle you or make you feel insecure, but to help you realise that change isn't bad or scary – again, it's an adventure!

Now, of course, some people really excel at change. I know that I don't enjoy too much routine but I like some, so again knowing your limits is important. Then, when you want to take leaps and make big changes in your life, your mind has already become used to the idea and will feel less unsettled by it.

It is like when we panic before going on an overseas holiday because we're getting on a plane and that's not something we do every day. We don't get the same feeling when we hop on a train or into our car; we do it every day so our mind doesn't find it a threat. If you are an avid traveller or frequently travel abroad for business then you wouldn't think twice about boarding a plane. It would be an everyday occurrence and you would simply get on with it.

LEARNING TO MANAGE CHANGE

Start effecting simple changes in your life every day. Don't do so much that you scare the heebie-jeebies out of yourself, but take a step-by-step approach. Start by considering your tolerance for change and then experiment – perhaps by walking a different way to work, or simply trying new foods to help you get into the groove of applying simple changes to your life. Then when you start to make bigger changes in your life, you will feel a little more comfortable and relaxed about it. Aim to bring about some small changes in your life with a little bit of grace and ease before you reach the end of the book.

You need to know what works for you

The journey you are about to begin is a personal one and, having helped hundreds of clients, I have found that one particular set of techniques or tools doesn't fit all. Some people prefer questions to help spark their change, while others prefer to take action or simply need time to reflect on what is being said. So really take your time to think about the way you like to learn and what will work for YOU.

Remember, what worked for your friend or colleague might not work for you too. Yes, your friend might have had great success with an acupuncturist, but you may find that either the therapist isn't working for you or you don't like the treatment. That is fine, and it is not a reflection on you – it just means that it wasn't the right therapy for you. We have to find our own journey and what works for us.

I described earlier in the book how there are 'no new problems,' but I trained in a number of different therapies because, along my journey, I found that people didn't respond in the same way, even when they seemed to have similar problems. When dealing with physical ailments, for example, I found the same two people could have headaches but one would benefit from massage and reflexology while the other would benefit from talking about it and releasing their stress that way.

As you work your way through the following chapters, you'll find that this book is full of questions to help you understand what your process is, and then help you discover the right route for you. So don't compare yourself with your friends and family because they will react in different ways.

I am an emotional person so crying is an important part of transformation for me because it helps me to find a release. Others may prefer to get angry and want to stomp, or dance, while others are more creative and like to paint or write. So not one thing will change you, there will always be a combination of things that will help. And that is why it is important to understand who you are and what works for you. You are unique and will deal with and process things in the way that is best for you.

You are unique. Embrace it.

I believe that is why my family fell apart after my sister died: we didn't grieve in the same way; we didn't deal with tragedy and loss together because we couldn't. We all had our different processes and this is what got us through it, however it divided us as a family.

Be brave and take a stand for your way. By all means take guidance from the others and this book, but ultimately you have to make it work for you.

AFFIRMATION

'I am responsible for my life.'

Chapter 3

Awareness Leads to Transformation

We all have a story and a catalyst for 'why' we need to change. It might be a simple event or a huge, life-changing one. The precise nature of your issue – whether it is battling for your life with cancer or other disease or just feeling lost, burnt out, don't like your job or dealing with a relationship break-up – is insignificant. Your issue might not seem as important as other people's but to you it is a huge change – so own your story, it is yours and whether it is big or small it is significant to your growth.

We need challenges to help us grow as human beings and if we see these events as wake-up calls to grow, to go in a different direction and become stronger, we realise that we can deal with anything.

This is really the first important step to change and something that people often don't take the time out to do and then wonder why they don't change. So without judgement bring some awareness into how you got here.

How did you get here?

Think about it. Have you ever driven somewhere and arrived at your destination then wondered how you got there? Sometimes life can be like this too. You wake up one morning and realise that you are not happy and say to yourself, 'How did that happen?' What we often fail to see is that it has been building up over time and we haven't listened to our feelings of feeling lost until that 'brick wall' moment hits us.

I believe that this is when we finally wake up. We become conscious of our feelings and our thoughts, and more often than not we know that our lives have to change.

KICK ASS YOUR LIFE

Over the years I have noticed how many people walk around unaware of what is happening to them, something perhaps as a therapist I can see more clearly than they can. They are not tuned into their bodies, their emotions or feelings. They only notice when things are going wrong and feel like it has just fallen out of the sky. Through my years of growth and expansion one of the best bits of advice that I received was,

It never just falls out of the sky.

There is *always* a build-up, you just haven't noticed. Although I have a pretty big story to tell – and I hope you never have to experience the same – I thought that my life was pretty good before it happened and nothing untoward had ever happened to me. But when I took time to explore where I was, I began to notice the things that hadn't been working before my sister died. That event was my wake-up call and, although I have hit the brick wall many times since, I've learnt to listen to the warning signs and take action before I hit burnout.

Case Study

A client came to me with severe migraines and was in constant pain. She said they appeared to have 'just come on', so I asked her if she had ever had headaches before. She said she had. I asked her what her story was and found that her migraines were her brick-wall moment. Her headaches were already telling her to stop, to take a moment to really see where she was: they were her warning signs and she ignored them. She needed to take a moment to release the pain of her relationship break-up, which was at the core of the problem (again the problem is never the presenting problem). She had an 'aha' moment and realised that she had been avoiding the pain on all levels.

When she bought awareness to her warning signs, they made more sense to her. She stopped trying to fix her headaches and instead looked deeper at the core of the problem. She now knows what her warning signs are and takes action before she hits her brick wall.

Awareness is the key to any 'aha' moment.

Every person has their own warning signs and once you become aware of what they are then you begin to notice when they are happening. The more you face your pain and feel in control, the easier the transformation.

If you don't take notice of the warning signs, they knock harder

Again the key is to be aware, don't run from them, just try and understand the deeper problem. Look out for any physical signs or feeling tired, as these symptoms will have a message. The following visualisation can help you learn to recognise what is going on inside. You might find it helpful to record the visualisation and play it back to yourself or simply read through it a couple of times before starting. Happy tuning in, but don't forget we are not trying to change anything just yet.

VISUALISATION 1 – TUNE INTO YOUR BODY
Find a quiet place to sit and be still.

Place your feet firmly on the ground and take a deep breath in and out.

Releasing all your tensions when you breathe out.

Breathe in and out.

Breathe in and out and begin to notice what is happening in your body.

First tune into your head and your neck.

Are your muscles tight or relaxed? Do you feel yourself holding tension in your neck?

Move your neck and see if you can find a more comfortable position.

Become aware of the thoughts in your head. Just be comfortable with them; you are not trying to change anything.

Become aware of them – how they chatter on, what are the quality of those thoughts

Does your head feel full or empty?

Just notice what is happening. Don't try and change anything.

Now move on down through your body,

Begin to notice your shoulders

Do they feel tight or relaxed? Move them around and tune into how they feel.

Now become aware of your chest and your breathing. Tune into how your chest is feeling, is it tight or relaxed, is your breathing deep or shallow. Don't try and change anything, we are just learning how to tune in.

Then come down and tune into your stomach.

How is your stomach feeling? Place your hands on your stomach and tune into what your stomach is trying to tell you.

Your emotions are normally stored there so tune into your feelings.

How are you feeling today? What emotions are being stored there today? Just notice them, without judgment. It is ok to feel these emotions. They are just feelings and they have no power over you.

Take time to tune in and to notice what is going on.

Everything is OK, you are feeling what you need to feel right now and that's ok.

Now tune into your legs – are they feeling tight or relaxed? Are they hot or cold?

How are your muscles feeling?

Tune into your calves and then into your feet.

Tune in as you go as to how every part of your body is feeling.

We are not trying to change anything.

Notice how that feels, are you wanting to change something, or do you feel happy and relieved that you don't have to change anything just yet?

Feel at peace with whatever you are feeling and noticing.

Take a deep breath in and out.

Gently wiggle your toes and fingers and when you are ready open your eyes.

Afterwards, take time to write down in your journal and describe how you were feeling and what you noticed.

You can use this visualisation every day if you wish but try to do it at least once every week and make sure you note down any changes or observations. Just tuning in really helps you to be aware of what is going on.

It didn't just fall out of the sky

As I said earlier, I often hear clients say that their feelings have just fallen out of the sky or they didn't see it coming. I can guarantee you that this is never the case; there has always been a build-up. It's about tuning in and recognizing the signs. Try and think back, and ask yourself: 'Did you feel lost before but didn't act upon it?'

It is really important to become aware of how you got here and to acknowledge where you are right now, and sometimes this is easier when we get down and dirty with our story. As I said before, this is not about self-blame and feeling guilty but about bringing awareness to your story so you see the light at the end of the tunnel and then find a way out.

Awareness is the key step to transforming whatever you want to change – to finding clarity about why you are lost. However, it's also the step that most people don't do because they are too scared to actually look at where they are, or how they got here because they believe if they don't acknowledge it, then it's not actually happening or the fear kicks in.

How do you know you are avoiding being aware?

Simply you find yourself doing something different, and you may find you are easily distracted from the task in hand. For example, when I was writing this book, the washing up (which I hate) or laundry became my number-one priority rather than sitting down and actually finishing writing the book. You too may have the same feelings that there is something more important to do than taking the time to explore where you are or feel you are too busy to take any action.

Not taking this step is detrimental to your transformation – to finding yourself and not feeling lost. After all, you wouldn't plan a train trip and say "I want to get to London" and then not state the station you are departing from. The same goes for transformation. If you are blinded even to the fact that you don't know where you are, then you won't be able to see where you are going either. This will leave you feeling frustrated and wondering why you can't change.

Sometimes I feel like I want to be somewhere different, so I don't have to deal with it but if I do I will bypass what I need to learn. I advise my clients not to leap from where they are to where they want to be because they won't learn how they got there – and then may end up right back where they started with no clue about how to change. That is why it is very important to bring awareness to your life.

The pitfalls

It feels right for me now to let you know the pitfalls of transformation and why people don't change, so that you are able to spot the signs as you venture into your story and avoid becoming a victim of your pain and staying there. So think of the following information as helping you to explore how you got to this place – of feeling lost, angry, scared and frustrated – and bringing more awareness to your life.

If you don't know where you are, you can't possibly move to where you want to be. Most people don't like to see where they are because sometimes it is too painful to realise that they have messed up or it is too emotionally raw to admit that they are feeling this way. Just remember, this process is not about blaming anyone or anything but rather observing and being non-judgmental of where we are.

Awareness can lead to transformation.

If it helps, you can try and imagine that your story belongs to someone else, a close friend perhaps, and this will help you to see it in a neutral light, without any emotions or feelings clouding it. That is why most people turn to someone for help. I can certainly see the amazing person in my clients but also where they are, and where they need to go before they are able to see it, because I am not emotionally attached to their story.

Pitfall 1: Fear

You already know that most people are fearful of change. Some don't like any change and would rather stay where they are. Some know they want to change but don't know how, and lack knowledge and understanding about how to change. I didn't know how to change either, and needed people to teach me and help me to understand what was going on, how my body was reacting and how to move forwards.

There is no shame in asking for help and sometimes when I meet people and tell them I am a coach or a therapist, they seem to move away pretty fast, saying 'I'm OK, I don't need help.' Help is seen as a sign of weakness but let me tell you that asking for help is more courageous. So *you* are one of the courageous ones, wanting to know the answers and taking a chance. As I described earlier, a huge weight lifted off my shoulders when I asked my acupuncturist for help.

Fear keeps us in the same place we were before. It keeps us small and doesn't allow us to grow. Fear will always pop up when we are going through any kind of change. But let me tell you:

Fear is a load of bollocks!

Having moved past fear many times let me tell you what will happen when you move past it. What will happen when you move beyond this imaginary line?

Honestly?

NOTHING!

Fear may make you feel a little nervous or a little sick but that is IT! Let me tell you a story of how I moved past fear and nothing happened so that you know that this is the truth.

I was at a conference and was asked to take part in a trance dance, something really unfamiliar to me and scary! After some encouragement, I decided to take part. I was in a room with around six other people and the teacher said that we needed to put on blindfolds, do a breathing exercise and then dance to the music. I was petrified! I put on my blindfold and started the exercise. Breathing in and out, I felt panic starting to rise but said to myself, 'I can leave if I want to, just walk out the room.' But something held me back and when the breathing got too much, I simply stopped and then started again. As I continued, I felt something in me move past the fear and the feeling turned into excitement of trying something new. The music started and I danced. I truly felt free as I moved beyond the fear barrier.

So when clients now come to me and say they are fearful, I share the story above. When we move past fear and nothing happens, we are less fearful next time. The thing to know about fear is:

Fear holds us back

Before I moved past fear I waited for the inevitable to happen and what I call the dreaded 'What ifs', which go something like, 'What if…'

- 'I can't do it?'

- 'I don't like it?'

- 'I fail?'

- 'People judge me?'

The 'what ifs' normally go on and on and on… BUT I did it, I moved beyond fear and I really enjoyed the new experience of trance dancing. I felt better and stronger and more confident in myself because I'd moved past fear. This also gave me evidence that I could do something new and this strengthened me.

Moving beyond fear strengthens you.

Many of my clients have experienced this line of invisible fear too and report that the same thing happens. It is the thinking about the fear that actually keeps you stuck and the inevitable 'what ifs'.

Pitfall 2: The pay-off

Another pitfall that I commonly see in my practice is that quite often we are actually getting something out of feeling lost. That doesn't mean we are feeling this way intentionally but unconsciously it is serving us in some way. For example, we might be,

- Getting more attention.

- Find that friends and loved ones are doing things for us.

- Receiving more love.

Case Study

One of my clients was poorly and having issues with her back. She wanted to know why she wasn't getting better, so we dug deep and found that her daughter had become more attentive (something that she wanted) since her back problem had started. Her daughter would come round and take her shopping and, more importantly, when she was really feeling down her granddaughter would visit her to cheer her up.

*This precious time spent with her family was obviously
something she didn't want to change so we worked out
another strategy. My client asked her daughter if she could
spend more time with her granddaughter by taking her out
and so on. Her daughter was delighted and my client's back
felt much better. She became unstuck in a matter of weeks.*

So you see how powerful the pay-off can be, even if it is not intentional. We love to feel that we are wanted more and so our body finds a way of getting that attention. If you are kinder to yourself then your body won't seek that attention because you are simply giving it to yourself. As human beings we crave love and attention, however, it is something we need to be able to give ourselves.

Pitfall 3: Don't become a victim of your story

As I said at the beginning, you are bringing awareness to your story so that you can transform it. But in doing that, you need to take care that you don't give it any power or judgement over you.

In the many years that I spent blaming external things and other people for how I was feeling, I remained in pain and was the victim. No matter how much healing I gave to the situation, it didn't change because I wasn't taking ownership of it and felt angry and resentful. When we are in this victim space, we cannot transform our story because we're clouded by negativity and can't see the light at the end of the tunnel. When we are in victim mode we feel disempowered and cannot transform what needs to change.

Becoming a victim to our story is a very common problem. I know that I have become a victim on many occasions, rather than really being aware of what I was doing. However, while it is difficult to rid yourself entirely of the victim mode, you can become more aware of it and learn to recognise it when it pops up in your life. With practice you can perhaps spend just 10–30 minutes in this mode before recognizing it, rather than a whole week, month or year!

When we are in victim mode it takes away our power therefore we cannot transform ourselves. We are giving our power away and hoping that someone else or something will fix it. Don't forget no one is coming to save you.

By becoming aware of what you are doing, you will learn to recognise this victim mentality. We can only transform things that are inside of us. I see many clients spinning around in circles trying to change others, getting burnout and then ending up not changing anything. We cannot change the external things but by changing our perception of it then change can happen almost instantly.

How can you recognise it?

You will notice when you are in victim mode because you will start blaming things or people (I call these external things – which you cannot transform). You might say things such as:

- 'It's my husband's/wife's fault.'

- 'I don't have enough time.'

- 'If I had enough money then I would be happy.'

- 'If I didn't need the money then I would have a better job.'

When things go wrong becoming aware of what you say, listen to the language that you use. You may feel overwhelmed and it will seem like you are spinning round and round, unable to get off that hamster wheel. When you are in victim mode you will tend to self-sabotage your success. You will beat yourself up a lot by being negative or saying negative things to yourself. You may start eating more, drinking more and not sleeping – abusing your body. To help yourself out of this situation, you need to look after yourself and by doing something physical like eating healthy foods and taking time out to relax will help you get out of this pitfall faster. Try not to judge yourself too harshly, bring love and compassion to yourself instead.

What happens when I go into victim mode?

I have transformed this part of my life very well although, as I said before, I do occasionally get into this victim space. I think it is a natural thing to do but simply being aware of it brings the biggest transformation.

Case Study

I had one client that wasted a lot of time in victim mode. She would spend up to a week feeling sorry for herself and therefore disempowered to make changes. She felt this was OK but when she started to realise that it was slowing down her transformation – and so making it harder for her to manifest the job and boyfriend she really wanted – she decided to make a change. She became aware of when she was in victim mode and then only allowed herself one day to feel that way and then the next day she continued with her transformation. This worked well for her because she gave herself permission to feel like this but only for a short period of time.

Again it is not a question of you never falling into victim mode but how long you are going to stay there. The more aware you are of it the less time you spend in this place!

Pitfall 4: Don't be hard on yourself

I tell my clients, 'Put the sticks down NOW.' Don't beat yourself up about where you are. You may feel disappointed and hurting that you have allowed yourself to get into this state. You may be feeling like you have failed, are out of control, can't possibly get yourself out it and will feel lost forever, *but* keep remembering that this is a process of exploration *and not* about beating yourself up. When speaking to yourself, remember this:

> *If you wouldn't say it to your best friend, then don't say it to yourself.*

We are the first to put negative emotions on ourselves – guilt, shame, anger – but this will not bring clarity to the situation, it will just cloud it even more. We are indeed our own worst critics.

> *Feel excited that it can only get better and it will.*

Pitfall 5: Your past has moulded you, but not defined you

As a therapist I tend to look back at my client's past but only briefly because, again, we are not trying to fix the past or you! A lot of therapies will heal your past but I find this is the longest route you could possibly take. I am always looking for the fastest route to change. After all, why spend years being where you don't want to be when you can look forwards to the future and start moving towards it.

But the past holds a lot of information and studying it or becoming aware of it can help you heal. It might be a major single event or something such as how your family behave – whether it's your mum, your grandmother, aunt, brother, sister or anyone that has a strong connection with you. Even your husband may bring out the worst in you, so become aware of what is happening there. It seems that our family often has special buttons that when pressed bring on our emotions, and particularly those seemingly bad emotions such as hurt, anger, resentment and generally feeling pissed off.

Although it can be difficult to go there, we can learn a lot about ourselves by looking at our family. The important thing to remember when thinking about their behaviour is to consider its influences on you without getting too emotionally attached or involved with it.

If it is learnt – you can simply unlearn it.

You can see how your past can really damage your progress to transforming your life because you can't change what you don't know. Just keep reminding yourself that the past does not define who you are, it just helps you recognise learned patterns that you need to unlearn.

Sometimes you can't see your own fears but by taking a closer look at your parents and family you can get a great deal of information about what your fears and anxieties might be. This all forms part of understanding yourself better and becoming aware of it so that you can transform it. (You'll find more on this in Chapter 4.)

If we believe we can change, we will.

Taking the next step

Don't forget that the pitfalls will slow down your transformation so read them carefully. Be courageous and take the next step towards transforming your life. As you continue on your journey, keep in mind the following:

- **Be aware.**

- **Take responsibility.**

- **Take action.**

You are well on your way to transforming your life with ease and grace so keep up the good work. Let's continue to kick ass your life!

AFFIRMATION

'I am willing to change.'

Chapter 4

Where Are You Now?

We have gone through the questions of why you want to change and you have familiarised yourself with the rules and pitfalls, so now it is time to bring awareness to your life by understanding where you are right now. Why is this so important?

If you don't know where you are right now, it's impossible to get to where you want to be.

GAINING SELF-AWARENESS

Whip out your journal and spend a few minutes considering each of the following questions and writing down your observations. Ask:

- What is my story?

- Does my past shed some light on my present situation?

- How did I get here?

- Were there any warning signs? If so, what were they?

- What am I getting by staying this way?

Be truthful and write down your answers in as much detail as possible. Don't forget, if you don't know where you are, you can't transform it and move forwards.

Don't forget these feelings didn't just fall out of the sky. They have built up over time and the more self-aware you become about the reasons 'why' so the easier it will be to transform your core issues.

Sometimes we don't notice the signs the first time but then something else comes along to knock us even harder into awareness. That's why understanding what is going on is really an important place to start.

Don't analyse the crap out it

My favourite word used to be 'why' and I would ask it of everything, yes I mean everything. I would ask, 'Why am I doing this?' or 'Why do I feel like doing this?' and 'Why don't I want to do something about it?' By the time I'd finished analysing it, I would normally lose the plot or the passion to do anything at all. Trying to work out why you are here, what happened and trying to analyse it will only do one thing: keep you exactly where you are!

That is why I believe the usual holistic route of trying to heal your past is sometimes too long-winded and can take many years of counselling and/or therapy. We just need to be aware of our story, we don't need to analyse it? So, what's the difference?

- **Awareness = Shining a light on you and the situation. Bringing compassion and love to it.**

- **Analysing = There must be something wrong. You are trying to fix something.**

- **Can you see and feel the difference? When you bring awareness to your life, you start to think of yourself as your best friend would. You remain unattached to your feelings and thoughts around it. This is not about bypassing your emotions, but disengaging from them so you can view them with a fresh perspective.**

Don't fall into the pitfall of beating yourself up!

If you are still finding it difficult to bring awareness to the issue without analysing or judging it then use the exercise below.

TIME TO GO WILD

OK, just for 10 minutes, give yourself permission to analyse the crap out of your story and where you are. Get a timer, no more than 10 minutes, and write it all down. If you're not sure where to start, here follows a few questions to help you.

- How the hell did I get here?

- What is the message?

- How have I got myself into this?

- Why do I feel so lost?

- Why are people around me so cruel?

- What did I do to deserve this?

- Why am I such a failure?

Ask any further questions that spring to mind, and keep writing until you hear the timer ping. Then immediately answer the following questions. Don't think about them too hard; just write down your first response.

- Did analysing the situation make you feel better?

- Was it a productive 10 minutes?

- Was it a waste of time?

- Did you achieve anything?

I don't know what you've written but I am pretty sure that your answer to those final four questions above was a big fat, 'NO'.

What's more you might feel even worse and still can't really see what the problem is. Am I right?

If the above exercise left you feeling confused or worse, I am sorry for doing that to you. Now try shining a light on you and the situation and feel the difference.

VISUALISATION 2 - SHINE A LIGHT

Find somewhere to lie down or sit comfortably where you won't be disturbed. Place your feet firmly on the ground.

This is time for you - to shine a light on your problems. You are safe and totally supported.

Take a few deep breaths and let your body and mind relax.

Breathe in and breathe out, releasing all of your tension as you breathe out.

Breathe in and breathe out.

In your mind's eye, see yourself sitting in a comfy chair.

Imagine a warm glow of love surrounding and protecting you.

You feel safe and supported.

Imagine that you have become a separate person standing beside the *you* in the chair.

You are now observing the old you in the comfy chair. You are totally unattached and just an observer. You are not feeling the pain of the old you.

The old you has come to shine a light on all of their problems and worries. It is safe for the old you to express themselves. They are totally supported.

As the observer, you see the old you through a new light.

As a great friend that needs comforting with love and compassion.

Allow your observing self to hear the woes and troubles of the old you with no judgment. They have no power over you. You can see these troubles in a new light.

As the observer you just need to be supportive and allow your old self to talk. All the old self needs right now is love and compassion and to feel that they are being heard and understood in a compassionate way.

Allow your old self to tell you about the things that are troubling them and making them feel lost for a few moments longer.

The observing you listens with a new understanding through a new light. The old you wants to be heard and comforted. The observing you listens with love and compassion.

When you both feel ready, say to the old you "I hear you". Gently encase them in a big hug. If the old you wants to cry and release all those pent up emotions then allow them to do so, without judgment. You are there to support your old self, not to judge.

As the observer tell the old you that you love them and will also support YOU even when things seem to be going wrong.

Allow both of you this time and space to be where you are and to be ok with this. Be in this space of love for each other, for a few more moments.

Enjoy this time to shine a light on whatever is happening at this time with no judgment and attachment. It's all ok.

Be safe in the knowledge that these fears and worries will change.

With a new understanding of yourself, imagine stepping back into the YOU in the comfy chair. You are now one but with more love and compassion for yourself.

You can now see that your feelings of being lost are not as powerful as you first thought, you can see that you have the power to overcome these feelings. There is light at the end of the tunnel.

Tune in to whatever you are feeling, it is all ok. You are safe and supported.

Take a deep breath in and out.

Gently wiggle your toes and your fingers, and then when you are ready open your eyes.

Did you notice the difference between having self-awareness and analysing. Awareness is 'shining a light on to your problems' in a non-judgemental way – in a loving and supporting way. This shouldn't leave you feeling worse or confused, and the next time you start analysing you will hopefully remember to stop and bring awareness to it instead.

If you analyse your situation, you can't transform it – you just fall into victim mode.

Your past influences you, it doesn't mould you

How would you feel if you didn't have a past? I have always thought this was a scary thought because I do want a past so that I can learn from it. Acknowledging our past and healing is very powerful, as it changes everyone around us; we are not just healing ourselves. Here follows a few guidelines to help you get you through this part of your story.

1. It is not hereditary

Behaviours are not hereditary, they are learnt, so feel empowered that you can choose to create a new behaviour and leave the old one behind. Don't live in your past, understand it, give it no judgement and then move forwards.

Case Study

I remember seeing a client with IBS (irritable bowel symptoms) and anxiety. She said everyone in her family suffered with this condition and believed that it was hereditary, which left her feeling powerless – she'd accepted what she thought was the truth. When I explained to her that it was a learnt behaviour, this was how she learnt the behaviour of having anxiety whenever she felt stressed or anxious and it was just a reaction, she was relieved to know she was in control and so could change it.

2. Acknowledge your past

Don't run away from your past because it has some really good messages that can help you transform and move you forward on your journey. Sometimes when we feel that our past is too much to bear, we feel overwhelmed and it gets us down. We might disconnect from life because we feel as though we can't change it. Don't be frightened of your past, even if something bad has happened. You don't need to relive the pain, you just need to bring a new understanding to it. Embrace your past, it has protected you thus far but in order for change it needs to be left where it is – in the past.

Case Study

I met one of my clients at a networking lunch. She asked me if I could help her with her hay fever. When I asked her, 'What else is going on?' she broke down in tears and said she was still grieving the loss of her mother who had died a year ago. The loss was so painful that she was trying to run from her past by saying that it didn't affect her anymore and so not allowing herself time to grieve fully. Finally acknowledging her true feelings, she was able to transform them.

3. Give forgiveness to your past

Don't be angry at your past and the people in it. It has very important information and for that we must be grateful. Sometimes when I see a client it is the anger and resentments that they are projecting towards their family, their relationships, or an event that's leading them to feel lost. However when we blame others, we don't own our part in it and, in order to heal the past, we must take responsibility for how we feel about it. Let me be clear, this is not about blame and whose fault it is, it is about acknowledging your past and letting it go. This is where we come from a real place of power and can transform the past by learning from it. If you are full of anger and resentment then you cannot transform the situation. We need to send forgiveness to everyone and, most of all, we need to forgive ourselves.

Case Study

One of my clients was having trouble in his relationships with his mother and brother, and wanted to understand how to have a better and more understanding relationship with them both. He explored the possibilities of how they might be feeling; of how they were living their lives and from the point

of view that they were doing their best. He simply forgave
them both for the past so that he could move on. The next
day, he rang to say that his relationship with his mother had
changed and he had even spoken with his brother after a long
period of silence. Simply by giving forgiveness he was able to
quickly transform his relationships with them both.

4. Your past didn't know any better

By healing yourself, you are literally changing your story and that of your past. Realising that your family, and their family before them, didn't know anything better – they were just following the same pattern as everyone else –helps us find compassion for them, which then makes it easier to move forwards and heal this aspect of our lives. Just thinking they didn't know any better can lead you to feel compassion and not anger (which of course will keep you stuck).

Becoming a parent helped me understand my parents more, and I sometimes hear myself say to my children, 'You didn't come with a manual.' I'm simply doing my best with the information I have at the time; the people who have hurt you in the past were doing the same. Try and see the problem from their perspective and how your parents were brought up. You will be able to see a human side to them all, we are not perfect and we all make mistakes.

5. Give thanks

It is not always easy to move away from the past when we have been living in it for a number of years. However, we forget to give thanks to our past: for bringing us to this point in our lives and allowing us to realise that things need to be different. If we don't have a past then how can we improve on it and know that we want something different or that we need new information.

Also, on some level, that story has kept us safe and inside our comfort zone. When we realise that we want to step out of our past and live a better life then this comfort zone is compromised. We may feel fearful but any change can feel scary, however, it is always worth it and the biggest step is often the decision to heal the past.

Feeling emotions such as anger, resentment and hurt will keep you feeling stuck. Doing something different – by giving thanks – gives us a new perspective and a more loving thought. Acceptance will enable you to transform it.

Doing the same thing will leave us with the same results.

Try something new and see how it goes.

Healing the past

If you are reading this book, then it's likely that you've already made the decision to confront and heal your past, and so will start to move forwards with ease. However, despite doing this work, you might find that you need to be aware of past feelings and events because they do sometimes bite us on the backside again. So it is important to continue to heal the past whenever it arises, as there are often many layers to it. You can spend many years in therapy going over and over your past but I believe that this is unnecessary. It's about acknowledging and becoming aware of your past while not falling into the pit of your past and the hurt it caused.

You can choose whether your past is going to affect
you or not. There is always a choice.

The following visualisation will show how easy it can be to heal your past. It came to me when I was healing a client and proved to be powerful for her and I have since used it many times to help others heal their past too. Don't let fear stop you; it's your choice, so give the visualisation a go and just see what happens.

GIVING UP THE STORY OF YOUR PAST

First, ask yourself, 'Are you ready to give up the story of your past?'

If 'yes', why?

If 'no', why?

Acknowledge your fears for a moment. What feelings arise when you think about giving up your past? Do you feel fear? Bring awareness into how you are feeling and write it down in your journal. Now use the following visualisation to help you release your past. Bundle up all your fears and anxieties and the feelings of being lost and let it all go.

HOW TO USE THIS VISUALISATION

You can do this visualisation as many times as you like. As I described earlier, your past can creep up on you as you grow and move forwards in your life. You can't fully heal your past but the more understanding and awareness of the past, you have then the quicker you see the pitfalls and avoid them.

VISUALISATION 3 - GIVING UP YOUR PAST

Find somewhere to lie down or sit comfortably where you won't be disturbed. Place your feet firmly on the ground.

Take a few deep breaths and let your body and mind relax.

If you notice thoughts popping into your head, acknowledge them but don't follow them. Rest in this space for a few moments.

Breathe in and out, releasing all of your tension and thoughts when you breathe out.

Breathe in and out.

You feel safe. You are willing to go on this journey. You are willing to let go of your past.

In your mind's eye you see yourself sitting in a chair and next to you is a rucksack, you are going to fill it up with your past.

The things you want to let go of right now. You are willing to let them go.

Your past might include people, objects, events, words, thoughts or emotions that are no longer serving you.

It may be an event that has traumatized you in the past but you are willing to let it go as it is not serving any purpose right now. It is just keeping you stuck and feeling lost.

You are willing to let it go.

Take a few minutes to go ahead and fill up your rucksack with whatever it is. Is it a word, an object, a person or a feeling?

Think of anything that can go into that rucksack.

Be safe in the knowledge that you know what needs to go into the rucksack even if you can't express it. All is well.

Your intention is to put anything in the rucksack that is not serving you right now.

Take a few moments to fill up your rucksack.

Again, in your mind's eye, get up from your chair, pull the strings of the rucksack tight and clip the lid firmly shut.

Your past is all safe and secure in the bag, nothing will leak.

You pull it over your shoulders and put it on to your back.

You take a few moments to feel how heavy this bag is and what a burden it is to carry around with you all the time.

So now let's begin the journey of releasing your past by going for a walk. As you start to move off wearing your rucksack, you see a door appear. Open this door and walk through it knowing that you are safe and supported.

It may feel strange and fearful, or it may not, you continue on your journey as you feel this is the right thing to do. You are ready and willing to give up these parts of your past that are no longer serving you.

As you step through this door, you see a beautiful hill in front of you, surrounded by fragrant flowers and emerald-green grass, and start your journey by walking up the hill.

On the top of the hill, a magnificent tree is waiting for you and you're aware that this is a beautiful place. You see the beautiful flowers and feel this is the right place to put down your rucksack. Finally releasing these parts of your past.

You are ready and willing to let go.

Swing your bag off your shoulders and let it fall down by the tree.

Spend a few moments, giving thanks to your past and the lessons you've learnt from it.

Send the people and all that is in your rucksack, love and healing and feel grateful that your past has led you here. You are ready to feel free from the past.

Breathe a sigh of relief and notice how it feels to be without this load on your shoulders. Shrug your shoulders to see how free they feel.

Take a few moments to notice how much lighter YOU feel.

With the knowledge that this rucksack is in a beautiful place, turn around so that your back is facing the rucksack.

Now begin to walk away. You might find you can run or you might you feel heavy in your steps. It's all ok.

With every step you take you notice how much lighter and happier you feel without the past weighing you down.

You might like to skip, dance, run or even laugh. Enjoy this feeling of freedom for a few moments.

Celebrate you and your past. Celebrate that your past can no longer hold you back.

Take a deep breath in and out.

When you are ready wriggle your toes and fingers and open your eyes.

Well done for facing up to your past and deciding to release it. It is time for YOU to feel like YOU again. You are amazing and you can do anything you want to. Just believe in yourself and trust that you can do it.

AFFIRMATION

'I am willing to let go of my past.'

Chapter 5

What Do You Want?

How are you feeling? On a scale of 1–10 how amazing are you feeling now, with 10 being amazing and 1 being completely rubbish. Are you starting to feel excited about moving forwards?

You are already armed with your *why*, so now it's time to move into the realms of clarity and find out *where* you want to be in the future. You are also aware of the pitfalls, have bought awareness into your life and decided to heal your past. Now it's time for you to ask yourself, 'What do I want?'

You are the creator of your life so feel empowered to create the life you want.

I believe we are the creators of our lives. We are really good at creating the lives we don't want but haven't had much practice in living the life we do want. I see many of my clients living the life they don't want simply because they haven't asked themselves, 'What do I want?'

Not everyone takes the time to do this but it's vital to take time out and bring awareness to what we are creating with our lives. Don't be one of those people who say, 'I don't have time, I have a busy life' and wonder why you're not happy.

Why don't we ask ourselves this life-changing question more often?

When I see a new client, the first thing I ask them is, 'What do you want?' They often look at me blankly and really struggle to answer because no one has ever asked them before and they've never thought to ask it of themselves. It's not necessarily all about goal setting, as it goes deeper than that. Many people focus on, and often moan about, what they don't want –rather than what they DO want.

Of course, bringing awareness to what you don't want can be beneficial, because it means you begin to exclude unwanted outcomes, but focusing on them will never take you where you want to go.

We create what we focus on

Have you heard the saying, 'What you focus on is what you get'? You may have even experienced it when, for example, you were broke and focusing on your lack of money brought more of the same. Or you have a bad day and while focusing on what went wrong, everything else seems to go wrong too. We all have experiences like this.

It is sometimes scary to know that we have the power to create what we want. You may not have had a lot of practice of creating the life you want, but we can change this and it starts by asking the following question: 'What would your life be like if you created what you wanted? Would you be happy?'

Case Study

One of my clients is great at creating what she wants. She gets clarity on what she wants and it appears. While working with me, she decided she wanted to work with animals and have enough money to take time out to do that. We came to the conclusion that she wouldn't be paid for her work with animals because she didn't have any experience, but neither of us envisaged what happened next.

She wrote down what she wanted, 'to work with animals and earn enough money to pay my bills' but didn't put any attachment on when it was coming or what it would look like.

A couple of weeks later, she got a job at the zoo as a volunteer and regular contract work that paid her bills.

When you are clear on what you want, trust that it is coming without being attached to the outcome, you'll find what you need comes towards you.

It's time to become clear on what you want right now. It doesn't have to involve big-picture thinking or your life purpose, it's just about taking the first step and considering what you'd like rather than what you've got right now. Looking at a bigger picture is OK but can sometimes leave you feeling frustrated because, if you're anything like me, you'll want it all to happen today, or at the very latest tomorrow. So leaping too far into the future isn't such a good idea because it can make what we want feel unachievable and can leave you feeling overwhelmed and frustrated.

For example, it's like the so-called A-list celebrities that seem to leap to fame in a heartbeat. They seem to spring up onto our screens as if by magic by having hit number one with their single or own an empire before they hit thirty. But dig a little deeper by reading their biographies or listening to interviews and you'll find that they've usually worked hard to achieve their status or it has taken several or many years to get where they are. It's a bit of an illusion because we don't see their journey, which is why it's easy to believe that success comes literally overnight. It can leave us feeling frustrated that we are taking longer than others. It gives us a false perception of success.

It's the same thing when you move away from feeling lost. If you leap too far out in front then you won't see the steps you've already taken and won't believe what you want is possible. So I don't want you to leap too far just yet, don't forget:

It's a journey, not a destination.

It's likely that you're reading this book because you are feeling lost, scared or frustrated and feel there is more to your life, so let's focus on how you want to feel and what you want your life to look like.

HOW DO YOU WANT TO FEEL?

Find a quiet place where you'll be undisturbed for the next 10 minutes or so. Take out your journal and answer the following questions by giving the first answer that comes into your head. There is no right or wrong answer, just write down anything that comes into your mind. Don't analyse it and don't ask why, just write and let your excitement build. Ask yourself:

- How do you want to feel?

- What are your desires?

- What are you going to do with the rest of your life?

These questions may seem a little scary, but you might know instantly what you desire out of life. Most people simply want to feel happy in their lives and to be surrounded by loving people.

Or, if you struggled to answer these questions, you may prefer to start from what you wanted when you were a child – because that's often where you'll find your forgotten dreams and innate talents. I remember as a child, I would imagine teaching a roomful of people and that's precisely what happened when I woke up to what I wanted as an adult.

So remember back to when you were a child, and remember the games you liked to play and, for example, did you like playing with the medical set or the play kitchen, writing or singing; and did you prefer to be a leader, be with friends, or prefer to be by yourself? Your desires will have changed and developed but the basic concept will still hold true. So ask,

- What desires did you have as a child?

- What do you desire now?

- Would you love to live in a different country?

- Would you love a new job?

- Would you love to start a family?

Dreams

Have you ever watched the movie, *The Secret Life of Walter Mitty*? He dreamt about being an adventurer and then one day he took action and started living his dream. Like Walter, we can create in real life what we dream up in our minds. Did you know that your mind doesn't know whether it is real or fantasy? Therefore we can 'trick' the mind into believing a new reality. Dreaming puts us in a state of excitement, of possibility, of something better and is really important if we want to create something different for ourselves.

A lot of top athletes do this by visualising going over the winning line or seeing themselves accepting a gold medal. In other words, they dream about their success and what it means to them in order to help them achieve it.

I was often told off as a child for daydreaming but I still love to dream and, yes, some of the things I dream about have come true, not all yet but that's another book! Open up your mind to new possibilities, don't allow your negative mind to come in and tell you that you can or can't do it or bog you down in what's possible. Just allow yourself to dream and visualise the future you'd like.

Get out of your head and dream.

If you're still not sure what you want

Some people say that they don't actually know what they want. I find this hard to believe because the answers are always inside us. However, we need time and space to dig deep, stop and actually listen to what we want. So it's less a question of 'don't know', and more 'I haven't really ever taken the time to think about it and allow myself to dream and question what I'd love to do'. That is why I've given you some tools and questions to help you on your journey, but you need to give yourself permission to stop and explore.

Your dreams for the future may not come to you straight away but get excited about exploring what you want. Sometimes when I focus on what I don't want this leads me to further questioning. So start on the things that you know you don't want and turn these around. Don't start analysing them and beating yourself up about what you don't want, just let it lead to further questioning about exactly what you do want.

You do know what you want.

The more we say 'I don't know what I want', the more stuck we can feel. It's like being caught under a dark cloud; it blinds us to what is there, so whenever you get stuck, start saying,

I do know what I want.

Even if you don't, just keep repeating, 'I do know what I want', and you will find that cloud of negativity passes over and you will begin to see what you want. This may sound a bit confusing but trust me when I say there is nothing wrong with you, you don't need fixing and all the answers are within you. So therefore you must know what you want. Don't forget it might be new for you but the more you ask yourself the clearer it will become.

All the answers are within you.

Overcoming blocks

If you're still feeling doubtful that you don't know what you want, suspend disbelief and just try the following over the next week or so.

Keep asking, 'What do I want?

And answering, 'I do know what I want.'

Journal what comes up and get excited about the possibility of finding what you want.

Read on to find out what lies at the foundation of all of your problems and how to strengthen your core so that you can live the life you want free from limitations.

Affirmation

'I allow myself to explore the possibilities of my desires. I trust and believe in myself.'

Chapter 6

The Foundations

Do you remember the song that you probably sang at school about the man who built his house upon the sand and the rain came tumbling down and washed the house away?

'Everyone then who hears these words of mine and puts them into practice will be like a wise man who built his house on the rock. And the rain fell and the floods came, and the winds blew and beat on that house, but it did not fall, because it had been founded on the rock. And everyone who hears these words of mine and does not put them into practice will be like a foolish man who built his house on the sand. And the rain fell, and the floods came, and the winds blew and beat against that house, and it fell, with a great crash".

Matthew 7 : v 24:27

Over the past 10 years of helping people, I have seen how strong foundations can help us to create longer-lasting change and that is what I want for you. And, while I am not religious, the above story from the New Testament gives a great analogy because if you want to live the life you want, free of limitations, then you need to start with solid foundations. That way you'll be strong enough to face anything and build a successful life (whatever success means to you).

House of cards

When I first became a therapist I looked at my clients' problems rather than what was causing them. My clients would come to me with headaches, stress, and migraines, and feeling unhappy, lost, frustrated, and so the list goes on. I learnt to peel away the layers of the presenting issue like an onion. The problem with this, however, is that it takes a long time and I realised I was just dealing with the same problems time and time again. Also clients would often return at a later date with the same problem. This left me doubting myself as a therapist and questioning the career I had chosen. To put it bluntly, it frustrated the hell out of me! All I ever wanted was to help people to stop struggling and live the life they wanted, free from limitations.

This is where I had the notion of looking at people like a house of cards. You know those houses you might have built as a child using a pack of playing cards – move one of the cards and the whole thing collapses. Nothing ingenious but this is how I felt that I could, in fact, create a longer-lasting and faster change. I didn't want to peel away the layers of an onion, I wanted to find the core card at the bottom of the house and pull it to make the house of cards fall down.

This led me to start exploring what lies at the bottom of the house. Listening to clients, and hearing them describe their issues, I began to realise that the answer never lay in what they said but in what they *didn't* say. Time and time again, I found the same three elements were at the heart of the problem, no matter what the individual presenting issue was. I began to see a pattern and how we need to build these foundations, just like the man who built his house on the rocks, so that when the rain and wind comes (life's challenges) you are more solid in your being.

Now, as I said before, you are not broken so you don't need fixing, but there are three core issues and transforming them creates a solid foundation in our lives. Most issues stem from the same point and they all begin with 'self – it's easy as EBC

- **Esteem**

- **Belief**

- **Confidence**

EBC – the start and end of everything

At the core of everything, the bottom layer is all about YOU. If you remember at the beginning of the book one of the rules was:

You can only change one thing in life, YOU!

By starting to look at the problem, you bypass the onion effect and go straight to the core of the problem. Therefore this is exactly where I start looking at all my clients' problems and, of course, my own, while always remembering:

You are not broken

You just need to uncover who you really are and build strong foundations by working to increase your self-esteem, self-belief and self-confidence. If you don't build a solid foundation then you may just keep fixing what is wrong. Doing that takes longer and you're likely to find yourself in the same position again and again without a clue how to get out of it and create the life you want – the life you dreamt up in the previous chapter.

Case Study

One of my clients came to me for help because she was suffering with sleepless nights. We started by delving into what she wanted and what her dreams were, before moving on and working on her self-esteem, self-beliefs and self-confidence. She said she wanted to work from home one day a week but knew this wasn't possible in her industry. However, we worked on her self-confidence and within a few weeks she had the confidence to ask for what she truly wanted.

So let's look at EBC in more detail and why it's fundamental to creating our strong foundations.

Esteem

This is how you *feel* about yourself. Do you criticise how you hair looks or what you are wearing? Do you feel like a failure? Do you feel out of control? Are you worried about what other people might feel and say about you? How do you feel about your life? Are you OK with where you are?

Beliefs

What is the quality of your thoughts about yourself? What beliefs are you hanging onto that don't serve you? Do you believe that you are not good enough? Do you believe that you are inadequate? Do you believe you can't have it all? Are your beliefs about yourself keeping you stuck and unable to move forwards?

Confidence

How confident are you? Do you feel able to go into a room full of people? Do you have the confidence to ask for what you want? Do you have the confidence to go for your dreams? Do you believe you either have confidence or not? How confident are you about getting what you want?

WHAT'S YOUR EBC

On a scale of 1–10, with 1 being the lowest and 10 being the highest, score yourself on the following:

- How do you feel about yourself?

- What is the quality of your thoughts/beliefs about yourself?

- How confident are you?

Now, as you are scoring yourself on these, don't fall into the pitfall of being hard on yourself. These scores are an indication of where you are right now and give you helpful information so you can see how far you've travelled by the end of the book.

The three EBC questions can be applied to any situation that you are facing and can help you to see where you are. Your scores will go up and down, according to what you are doing and if you are stepping outside your comfort zone or not. For example, when you are at work these three questions might score highly but when you do something new or unfamiliar, then the scores may fluctuate and that is OK.

Whatever the scores are, accept where you are without denying or judging them. Be truthful and if your beliefs score is a three, that is OK; it's just where you are right now and is not an indication of the future. By bringing awareness, taking responsibility and then taking action you will be able to increase this score very quickly. If you don't then you will remain stuck. It's OK, this is the brave part and you can get through this.

Don't judge where you are; just accept it.

A score of 7 or above is pretty good and if it's any lower than that then don't worry because the exercises in Chapter 8 are designed to help increase your score so that you can move from feeling lost to feeling great.

Before we begin to build your foundations, first we need to explore who YOU are.

AFFIRMATION

'I am good enough.'

Chapter 7

Who Am I?

Even when we're aware of what the foundations are, sometimes we struggle to build them up because we don't know who we are, just yet. Don't worry because this chapter is all about finding out who you are and what your strengths and weaknesses are. So let's start by taking time out to explore who YOU are by asking:

- **Who are you?**

In order to begin to work with these foundations, the most important step we can take is to open our hearts to love and possibilities. Often our hearts are closed because of something that happened in the past, and it is therefore tricky to build self-esteem and confidence, and solid beliefs about ourselves.

Opening your heart

Is your heart open or shut tight? Trusting or mistrusting? When we open our hearts we come from a place of love, acceptance and forgiveness for all that we are. Unfortunately we are often too busy trying to protect our hearts from getting hurt, but this shouldn't prevent us from opening our hearts and finding love within it for ourselves. When we come from a place of love then people can feel and see that we are being authentic. Now this doesn't mean that you feel open to everyone and divulge absolutely everything about yourself; it means that you love yourself more while still protecting yourself.

I remember when I first went to see an osteopath because my shoulders and neck were painful only to be told that I was protecting my heart. I felt so relieved that someone understood me and the words struck me as being true: I knew the pain came from being hunched over and trying to protect my heart from being hurt again. When you experience any kind of loss, it is difficult to open up again to love, which is why it is so important to learn to open your heart and love yourself. Use the following exercise to help you experience more self-love.

Opening your heart allows us to receive love.

Visualisation 4 – Open your heart

Find somewhere to lie down or sit comfortably where you won't be disturbed. Place your feet firmly on the ground.

Take a few deep breaths and let your body and mind relax.

If you notice thoughts popping into your head, acknowledge them but don't follow them. Rest in this space for a few minutes.

Breathe in and out, releasing all of your tension and thoughts when you breathe out.

Breathe in and out.

You feel relaxed and safe to open your heart.

Pick a colour that represents love to you.

It could be pink or yellow, blue, purple or red - any colour you like. The colour that represents love to you

In your mind's eye, imagine a closed rose bud, the colour that you have chosen that represents love in the centre of your chest.

Imagine the rose bud beginning to open to become a beautiful flower.

Be safe in the knowledge that you are in a well-protected space. You are supported and loved.

Continue opening the bud and notice how you are feeling. Is there anything holding you back from opening this bud. Do you feel any resistance from allowing this bud to open.

You may feel vulnerable and a little scared, whatever you are feeling, it's ok.

Just notice how you are feeling.

Do you feel safe or vulnerable or a little scared?

As it becomes the beautiful flower, repeat the affirmation, I am willing to love myself just the way I am.

Visualise the beautiful rose in the centre of your chest and allow the colour to radiate all around your body.

Start at the top of your head, and slowly bring the feeling down to your shoulders, your arms and around your torso, down to your legs and ankles.

Just sit in this beautiful space and give love to yourself, to the change that you are about to instigate. Hold onto the feeling of love for yourself.

Opening your heart allows you to receive the love you deserve.

Bathe yourself in the colour of love.

When you are ready and in your own time, safely close the rose in your chest again until it is a tight bud. Remember any time you feel difficulty receiving love you can allow this rose bud to open and immerse yourself in the colour of love.

The more you practice receiving love the easier it will become.

Take a deep breath in and out.

When you are ready wriggle your toes and fingers and open your eyes.

When you open your heart you can then see yourself with love and compassion, the next exercise will be easy.

Stop listening to your head and listen to your heart.

WHO AM I?

Whip out your journal again and start a blank page with the words 'I am'. Be positive about yourself and see yourself in this new light of love, coming from your heart and not your head. Aim to write at least 10 'I am…' statements. For example, you might write,

- I am amazing.

- I am courageous.

- I am good at painting.

- I am great at cooking.

- I am happy.

- I am adventurous.

- I am beautiful.

- I am kind.

- I am loud.

- I am excitable.

If you're feeling stuck, ask your trusted friends. A couple of weeks ago my friend said I had a kind heart. I had never thought of that one before and it was a great compliment, so I immediately wrote down 'I am kind' in my journal.

When you feel like you have dropped into victim mode, or are getting down on yourself, this list will remind you of the authentic you – the truth of who you really are. It will help you feel uplifted even if you don't believe your 'I am… statements yet!

What are your strengths and weaknesses?

We all have strengths and weaknesses and once you realise what they are, you will begin to understand yourself better. We are not meant to be good at everything. I know that one of my strengths is that I love to create things, while one of my weaknesses lies in not knowing how to put my creations into action and if it's not new I lose interest. By acknowledging that I can't do it all, I've learnt to either delegate it to someone else or know that it's not one of my strengths and I need to be patient with myself because it may take more time.

You can do this exercise yourself but, again, sometimes your trusted friends and colleagues are better at identifying your strengths and weaknesses – so don't be afraid to ask them.

UNDERSTANDING YOUR STRENGTHS AND WEAKNESSES

Whip out your journal and make two columns – one for strengths and one for weaknesses. Every time someone gives you a compliment, this can go on your strength list or you might ask a friend,

- What am I good at?

- What comes easily to me?

- What are my natural talents?

- What do I struggle with?

Make up your own questions to suit you. By building on your strengths list, you gain confidence whereas the weakness column will help you to shine a light on the aspects of yourself where you need to be kinder to yourself because it is not one of your natural talents.

There are always some things other people are better at, so start by celebrating your strengths. Again, they won't be the same for everyone.

Everyone is different; you are YOU.

Now that you know who you are, let's work on building on your foundations so that you can be YOU.

AFFIRMATION

'I love myself just the way I am.'

Chapter 8

EBC – Building Solid Foundations

In the last chapter you learnt more about who you are, but sometimes we don't believe it or they are just words – but by working on your foundations you'll consolidate your learning about who the real YOU is.

In order to firm up your foundations, you need to discover more information about yourself: what you love to do and what you don't. Don't forget you are not trying to fix what is wrong because, you are not broken. As I described earlier, you are just revealing your true self, something you haven't probably been for some time.

Why do you need to build a solid foundation?

You may have heard other people say, 'I will do that when I have the confidence' or 'I will go and meet new friends when I feel better'. Before you make the mistake and fall down into the pit of the unknown, know that for most people EBC is built, it doesn't come naturally because we have never been told how to do it. Obviously we have more confidence and self-esteem when we do everyday things but when it comes to change we all feel a little wobbly when we step outside our comfort zone. I heard the following story which illustrates this point.

There was man who was really confident in his work. He was an expert salesperson and spoke at big conferences many times each year; this was his comfort zone. However, when he was asked to speak at his best friend's wedding, everyone was surprised that he crumbled; he was out of his comfort zone. Watching him speak, he sweated, was anxious and stumbled over his words – a shadow of his everyday professional self.

In the same way, trying something different may make you feel a little scared, lost, lacking in confidence but the more you do it, the more you get outside your comfort zone the more confident you will become. This goes hand-in-hand, of course, with thinking positively about yourself and feeling wonderful. So the more we love ourselves, treat ourselves with kindness and compassion, so we accept this is who we are. When we believe that we are good enough, then life gets simple and we can live the life we want free from limitations.

Live the life you want free from limitations

E – How do we build our self-esteem?

How do you *feel* about yourself? On a scale of 1–10, with 10 being amazing and 1 being rubbish?

Esteem is simple – you are at peace with yourself and don't make apologies for being you (now you know who you are) – even if you are awkward, nervous, noisy, excited, etc.

The first part of feeling good about yourself is to find out what makes you feel good, so if you feel lost again you can look back at your journal and pick one thing that makes you feel good. It may seem simple but when we're feeling frustrated, lost and down, it's hard to remember what makes us happy. This is why journaling every stage of these exercises will provide you with tools that will work now and be a valuable resource for the future. In essence you need to do things that fill you up and energise you.

WHAT DO YOU LOVE TO DO?

When I ask this question clients often look at me blankly and say, 'I don't know.' I appreciate that answering this question might not come naturally to you and might take some time to answer and that is OK. I know when my children were younger and I was trying to juggle children and work, I did actually forget what I loved to do. So this is great question to ask.

Just write this question on a fresh piece of paper in your journal and maybe add one or two things to your list every day. Don't analyse it too much, just go with what comes first into your mind. You might not even have done it yet but you may fancy doing it.

Then, at the next opportunity, start doing some of the things on your list. You have to do them because if you have forgotten what you love to do then it is only by doing them that you'll remember whether you like them or not.

You might like to start by looking at what you read, what magazines you buy, what you watch on the TV. These are all great starting points and will bring to light what you are most interested in. For example, I watch a lot of cooking shows, house improvements and wedding programmes! These are the things that light me up, that interest me. I don't know necessarily why, but I enjoy watching these programmes. I love to flick through a copy of *Vogue* and other fashion magazines. I love to see the latest fashions and feel the glossy pages.

Many people make a list of what they love to do but then don't take action. You MUST do something about it. If you don't take action then you can't move forwards or transform. You do need some movement, obviously in the right direction. That way, next time you start to feel bad about yourself you can choose to do an activity that you enjoy to help you feel good again.

Case Study

A client was really unhappy with her life, her relationship and her business. She had simply lost passion for her life.

She started by saying that she was leaving her relationship and walking away from the business that she had spent quite a lot of money on. I then asked her what magazines she read and what she was passionate about. She loved bespoke designs and realised that in her business she simply wasn't creating bespoke work. Once she realised what she loved to do, she booked onto a life-drawing course and began making more bespoke flower arrangements in her business. She began to regain passion for her life and business, which helped her feel more in control and thus much happier.

Why is it so important to do things you love?

A lot of the time we look to other people or to external things to makes us happy, or simply go along with things, unaware of how they make us feel. I believe you must first look at what makes YOU happy.

If I could redefine the word 'selfish' I would. I believe that we have to look after ourselves because then we are able to look after others. After all, you wouldn't expect your mobile phone to last for forty years without ever recharging the battery. It's the same for YOU. You need time to re-energise your life with things that make you feel passionate and vibrant.

When I ask my clients to do something for themselves, they often feel very guilty that they are taking time out or buying something for themselves. I know how they feel – particularly if they have a family or small children because I know it can be feelings of guilt that stop us from looking after ourselves. Eventually, however, when I did run out of steam and after hitting burnout several times, I realised how important it was to take time for myself. I now feel irritated if I don't get my fix, 10 minutes for myself every day. It took me a while to master it but I'm worth it! Like the L'Oreal hair advert:

You are worth it.

I can already hear you saying '... but I don't have time, I'm too busy.' I've heard it all before. The one thing you *have* to do is to *make* time. Mark out some 'me time' in your diary, if you need to make it happen. Even if it is 10 minutes reading a magazine in the garden or having a quiet cup of tea every day, that's all that it takes. Going to a spa is fantastic but you don't have to take a whole day, I would rather have time every day for me to recharge than wait once a year to relax when on holiday.

If you don't look after yourself, then you can't help others.

WRITING A HAPPINESS LIST
Answer these questions to help you remember what makes you happy.

- What 10 things do you love to do? (Just start with 10 things. If it doesn't come naturally, then take your time to consider your answer and add to your list over the coming days and weeks.)

- What makes you happy?

This is a powerful question to get you started, and don't forget you can add to your list whenever you remember something, so leave some space in your journal. You might even want to start collecting photographs and pictures from magazines or online, and positive quotes that make you feel good about yourself and your life. Put your collection of images together and create a vision board of all the things you love now and the things you want to try in the future.

Get passionate about your life.

If you don't know what you love, don't let that stop you

Take the time to really explore what you love. Go out and try something new or something you haven't done for a while and see how it feels. Did you love it? Or was it OK? Or more importantly ask, 'Did it recharge me?' Don't forget things that make you feel energised are key to improving your self-esteem and confidence.

Remember too, that it's important to find a balance of doing things with other people and things by yourself. I saw a client once and she would only do things with other people but not by herself. While this is OK, you need to be happy spending time with yourself so that you can understand yourself better.

What happens if I go off track?

I often hear from clients that they have done things in the past that haven't made them happy, simply to keep others happy. I know I do this, especially when my children are involved, but now I am more in tune with myself and know what I love to do so I am quite picky about what I choose. I ask myself some simple questions to keep me on track.

LIVING THE LIFE YOU LOVE
Bring more joy into your life by doing the things you love to do, not the things you don't. To keep you on track, apply the following simple questions:

- Do you feel safe and comfortable?

- Do you enjoy it?

- Does it make you happy?

- Do you want to do it?

If you get a 'no' to any of these then simple don't do it. Say "no" to the person who is asking you to do something. It is very simple but sometimes saying no is hard.

It does take practice but by checking in with yourself, you'll find that you start living the life you want and not one full of compromises that make you unhappy. Sometimes we need to compromise, of course, but constantly putting other people's happiness, or preferences above our own can leave us feeling really unhappy and frustrated. Don't forget, you are the star in your life, so start making decisions that make you feel happy.

One of the other keys to transformation is to simply be kinder to yourself.

Love yourself just the way you are.

As I said earlier, it is important to feel at peace with who you are. Are you loud? Are you excitable? Are you quiet? If you can't love yourself warts an' all, how can you expect anyone else to do it? You need to move through the cloud of being lost by being more loving and kinder to yourself and accepting your strengths and weaknesses.

PAMPER YOURSELF

Do you take time out for yourself? The best way to get back in love with you is by physically doing something for yourself, such as eating healthily, exercising or soaking in a bath with essential oils (I love lavender, geranium and rose!). These small, loving acts will help you feel more in control – even when really you feel lost or like you've hit a brick wall.

Sometimes when we feel stuck and frustrated, it's better to go out for a walk, do some gardening or hit the gym (if you're that way inclined) rather than sit at home procrastinating and worrying. Getting your body moving, in a way that you enjoy, is also a way of pampering yourself and can help you find a new, more positive perspective.

Loving yourself warts an' all is not a sign of giving up or accepting you are going to be like this for the rest of your life, even when there are some things you want to change. Rather it reiterates that you are not broken and so don't need fixing. Loving yourself just the way you are is more transformative than trying to fix yourself.

Loving you will lead to change.

Accept love from others

How do you receive compliments? Do you bat them away? Do you talk over them? Accepting compliments is sometimes difficult because we simply are not programmed to receive love from others. So when someone says, for example, 'Your hair looks nice today', start listening to what you say by way of return. Do you say, 'Oh I didn't do anything special' or 'I didn't really notice'. Did you notice which words are missing?

Thank you.

Yes, two simple words that we forget to say. Receiving a compliment is like receiving a gift from someone. When someone hands you a gift you don't give it back. You say 'thank you'. This may feel uncomfortable at first but get into the habit of saying 'thank you' every time you receive a compliment, it will help you recharge. You might want to write them down and re-read them when you are feeling lost to help you remember the truth: that you are, in fact, truly AWESOME!

B – What are your core beliefs?

What is the quality of your thoughts about yourself? On a scale of 1–10, with 10 being amazing and 1 being rubbish?

When we start to understand that how we act or respond to what is going on around us is down to our beliefs about ourselves, then they become a key part in our transformation. So what are core beliefs?

A core belief is a statement that resonates with you, that you feel is true about yourself and your life. However, most core beliefs are just myths. The truth is,

Most beliefs are not true at all.

Some beliefs you may have had for some time and come from your past. You are probably holding on to old comments you heard from your parents, caregivers and even your teachers when you were growing up. It took me years to realise that I held a core belief that I was stupid. When I explored the belief and looked for its source, I realised that a teacher had said this to me because I am left handed. Sometimes we don't realise how thoughtless comments can be installed in our belief systems, even when the original harmful comment was given unintentionally.

When we become more aware of our thoughts, we can easily identify any harmful or self-limiting core beliefs, even when they are subtle. Below are the most common limiting core beliefs that I hear from clients:

- I can't do it.

- I'm not good enough.

- I'm not worthy.

- I am insignificant.

- I can't have what I want.

- I can't say no.

- I'm not in the right place.

- I am not powerful.

- I can't show my true feelings.

- I'm not a good person.

- I can't receive love.

- I'm not attractive.

- I can't do what I want.

- I don't love myself the way I am.

- I'm not in control.

- I'm not in charge of my life.

- I don't deserve love.

- I can't to what I love.

Your beliefs about yourself have a direct influence on how you feel about yourself, so uncovering any that are preventing you from creating the life you want is an important step in the right direction.

TRANSFORMING LIMITING CORE BELIEFS

Whip out your journal and read through the list of core beliefs again. Ask:

- Which ones jump out at you?

- Which ones make you most uncomfortable when you read them?

- Which two common core beliefs do you identify with most strongly?

In my experience, most people have one or two limiting beliefs, which repeatedly come up in most situations. If you identify strongly with a number of the core beliefs, restrict yourself to just two to start with because trying to work on any more than that can leave you feeling overwhelmed or like you can't change them.

Remember, this is not about focusing on the negatives, but identifying what's holding you back so that you can transform it into something more positive.

Turning core beliefs around

Once you've identified your limiting beliefs, you can transform them into a belief that serves you better by using affirmations.

Negative belief	Positive belief
I can't do it.	I can do it.
I'm not worthy.	I am worthy.
I'm not in charge of my life.	I am in charge of my life.
Life is hard.	Life is easy.

For example, if you are going for an interview and you feel that 'you are unworthy' of getting the promotion or something better then create an affirmation that is either 'I am worthy' or 'I can do it'. Repeat the affirmation as often as you can during the day, and make sure it is the first thing you say to yourself when you wake up or before going to sleep.

You might not be aware of what the real core belief is but the more practised you become at identifying negative or limiting thoughts, the sooner you'll recognise any limiting beliefs that come up and start to turn them around.

Affirmations are more powerful when you put feelings into the words.

When you start putting affirmations into your life they can feel a bit flat and you may not be sure whether they are working or not. You may say the positive belief and it might feel untrue or as though you are lying to yourself. Don't forget your mind is plastic and has the ability to rewire its thought processes so you can literally programme your mind into believing the stated concept. Your mind doesn't know the difference between real or fantasy. However, it is important to put some feeling into your affirmations. So if, for example, you say, 'I can do it', without excitement or passion, then it probably won't be enough to turn the limiting belief around. However, if you say 'I love myself just the way I am' and dance around with the feeling that it is true then the affirmation will work its magic. Even dancing to music or purposefully walking while repeating the affirmation will elevate your feelings and help you believe in what you're saying.

After doing the 'transforming limiting core beliefs' exercise, add to your 'I am' list from the 'who am I?' exercise in the previous chapter. See how many you can add.

C = How to be more confident?

How confident are you? On a scale of 1–10 with 10 being amazing?

Confidence sometimes gets confused with self-esteem. Although there is a correlation between the two, I differentiate between them in the following way: self-esteem is a state of a mind whereas confi-dence lies in taking action.

Confidence grows when you take action.

Confidence grows when we know more about ourselves because we have brought self-awareness into who we are, know our strengths and weaknesses, and so know how to act in order to create the life we want.

UNDERSTANDING YOUR CONFIDENCE

We talked about comfort zones in Chapter 3, so let's find out when you feel confident and when you don't. Bringing awareness to your life can help you decide which are the right action steps to take, so ask:

- When do I feel most confident?

- When do I feel less confident?

Answer these questions by first asking:

- What am I doing?

- What activities scare me?

- Where am I?

Go into as much detail as possible and remember that confidence is built over time.

Once you have a list of what makes you feel less confident then you are ready to take action and face your fears. Of course, if you don't really want to do them, then don't. But if a lack of confidence is keeping you stuck and feeling lost, then proving to yourself that you can face them is the only way to overcome your fears.

You might want to start by trying one thing that you lack confidence in each week or each month, whatever works for you.

In this way, your confidence will grow over time as you start seeing evidence that you can overcome your fears. Evidence is built by taking action.

EBC as a whole

By building strong EBC foundations we can live a life free from limitation because when we have a strong core belief that we can succeed and then take action the outcome is bound to be more successful and that, in turn, increases our confidence. For example, if you have a strong belief that you can lose 10lbs, you will then feel good (even before you've lost the weight) and more encouraged to eat healthily and take exercise.

Loving yourself more makes it easier to reach your goals.

You cannot feel confident without self-esteem and strong beliefs, so in essence EBC works as a whole and you can use it to help you to transform anything in your life.

TIME TO REFLECT

Now you are getting to know yourself better, ask these same questions again:

On a scale of 1–10, with 1 being the lowest and 10 being the highest, score yourself on the following:

- How do you feel about yourself?

- What is the quality of your thoughts/beliefs about yourself?

- How confident are you?

Have your scores changed since you started this journey? Do you feel better about yourself?

Don't forget to keep journaling all the changes.

Next up, some more rules to help you live the life you want.

AFFIRMATION

'I trust and believe in myself.'

Chapter 9

Setting New Rules

As I said earlier, when you begin a new journey, it can feel scary. This is because you are creating a new set of rules for yourself. You are living by your own values. You have already figured out that living the way you are currently isn't helping you; it doesn't make you feel fulfilled or is simply making you feel stuck and unhappy.

When we set new rules for ourselves, which are perhaps different from the majority of our friends and family, this can make us feel a little uncertain or wobbly. These fears and feelings will come up, so allow them. Don't forget it's not that you won't ever feel like this again, it is how long you stay feeling lost. Just remember that it's OK because you are in the process of building stronger foundations for yourself.

Living by new rules – yours!

We feel lost when we use other people's rules and wonder why they don't work for us. Wonder why we don't fit in. You do know what makes you feel happy and confident but the rules we tend to follow are more usually set by society or by our families. They may have fitted us when we were younger but in adulthood they might limit us or leave us feeling trapped or stuck. In other words, our old ways of being no longer fit the life we want to live. So let's get creative and set up a few rules that will fit in with what you want and will help you to continue your journey towards living the life you want.

I believe that a big part of feeling lost is that we want different answers and new information that fits with how we want to live our lives. As I said in an earlier chapter, your friends and family may not understand that you are setting yourself some new rules and therefore you may need to seek out other people that are living the way you want to, more positively. I know that over the past 15 years of self-development, I found the process of transformation got much easier when I learnt to surround myself with like-minded people. You may also find, as I did, that you will be drawn to those groups of people that can help you feel more comfortable.

I know, even now, that when I create change in my life some of my acquaintances and friends will fall away or we'll lose touch, and that is fine. I simply see this as meaning that I will meet other friends who will support the change I am bringing into my life.

Case Study

One of my clients was trying to save for a house but she didn't seem very excited about the prospect of actually buying one. When we dug deeper, she realised that she wanted to travel and didn't want to be tied down to mortgage payments, so I asked her why she wanted the house. She told me it was 'the responsible thing to do', 'what other people were doing' and 'it would please her father'. When we explored this further, we discovered that these were the rules her father had imposed on her (albeit with the best of intentions) but it wasn't her dream.

So many people simply accept the beliefs passed on to them that they find it difficult to see how they might be limiting their ability to find happiness. I know that when I started working from home 19 years ago (which wasn't such a common practice as it is today) I could feel the negativity coming from others when I said I worked for myself and believed that others thought I didn't earn much money (which I did). In fact I was so wrapped up in what others thought of me that I missed the fact that I was living by my rules and had, in fact, found the perfect solution: a job that meant I could work flexibly and so spend more time with my children.

Growth and looking at ourselves is challenging but also fun if we approach it in the right way. I found change hard because maybe I was trying to hold onto a set of rules that no longer worked for me.

Have fun exploring your new rules. Be a trailblazer!

MAKE YOUR OWN RULES

Now it's your turn to make YOUR rules.

In your journal draw a line down the middle of the page and make two columns. Title the first one, 'Rules that don't fit with me' and the second 'My rules'.

You may find that you have a lot to add to the first column of rules that don't fit, and know that's OK. Doing this exercise the first time often kick starts a process that you'll need to keep coming back to over the coming weeks and months. As your list grows so your new rules will become clearer,

In setting your own rules you begin to understand your core values and this will help you live a more fulfilling life.

Core values

Core values are something that I teach all the time, especially to employees of large corporations. Of course, it's easier to live by our core values if you are running your own business or are self-employed. However, I believe when we cross or compromise our core values then this is where we become most vulnerable and are likely to get stressed out and ultimately experience burnout.

When we compromise our core values, we undervalue ourselves and this can leave us feeling unworthy, which obviously doesn't help our self-esteem or confidence because it gives us more evidence that 'we are not good enough'.

Everyone has a set of core values that they live by, whether they are aware of them or not.

Case Study

I gave a client an exercise where she would go to work and then ring me when some of her core values had been compromised. By 9.15 a.m. (she started work at 9 a.m.) she would text me saying that at least five of her core values had been crossed. No wonder she was feeling frustrated and felt as though she didn't fit in. After a short time she decided that where she worked no longer served her.

FIVE CORE VALUES

Take some time to make a list of your core values to guide you through certain situations and increase your sense of self-worth. Aim to list at least five core values in your journal. Examples might be:

- I loved to feel valued.

- My children are important.

- I value my time.

- I keep my house clean.

- I need to feel respected.

- I need to feel safe.

- I need to experience joy and fun.

Now ask yourself:

- How do I feel when my friends, colleagues, family or anyone else crosses these values?

- In what situations do I compromise my values?

Doing this exercise will give you a clear indication of whether you are in the right job or on the right path to living the life you want. Some of your values may change over time but I believe there is a set of core values that don't change. They become more important when you live by them. On the other side of the scale, however, if you don't live by your values and compromise them, then it will leave you feeling unworthy and simply SHIT about yourself.

Now you are armed with your core values, how will you live by them?

Start living the life you want – it's the only way!

AFFIRMATION

'I am safe to be me.'

Chapter 10

Your Journey So Far

On a score of 1–10, with 10 being excellent and 1 none at all, score yourself on the following:-

- **How do you feel about yourself?**

- **What is the quality of your thoughts/beliefs about yourself? Are there any beliefs that are holding you back?**

- **How confident are you?**

You may notice that all areas of your life are changing. You may feel more confident and stable in knowing who you are. Just keep in mind that transformation is a continual journey, so you'll keep taking strides forward and pushing yourself on to success. Whatever success means to you.

When you reach a plateau, don't think that this is the place to stop – this is only the beginning, the beginning of something much bigger than you are. Continue on your journey with the understanding that your foundations are getting stronger and stronger every time you become more of YOU, being in your power and, unapologetically, yourself.

Well done for doing the exercises to build your EBC foundations. Do you feel better?

Look back through your journal and review the journey you've been on. It's inspiring to think that by doing things differently, by changing the way you think about yourself, by loving and being kinder to yourself and taking action, you can start living the life you want. I am constantly amazed by the transformational stories that my clients tell me. No two stories are the same; your story will be different to mine and unique to you because the process of change is about finding what works for you.

CHART YOUR SUCCESS

Time to get out your journal and chart your success. Be honest with yourself and answer the following questions from your heart.

- Do you feel amazing yet? If not, can you see 'amazing' in your future?

- What have you learnt?

- Do your foundations feel stronger?

- Do you feel a little less lost than before?

- What steps have you taken to finding yourself?

- Do you feel like you have found what you thought was lost?

Change takes time

As I said at the start of this book, changing your life isn't just for Christmas. It is a lifestyle choice, so you might find the following hints and tips helpful in maintaining your positivity in the weeks, months and years to come. You need to build up your new muscles of thinking well about yourself, feeling confident and protecting your core values.

You can only go forward now.

You may slip a little but that is OK. Some people are scared of going back but I believe you can never go back. You can stay stuck but not go back. You have new information and understanding of who you are and hopefully you have some new tools to help you so that you can choose to live and think differently about yourself and your life. All you have to do is decide that you want to continue to move forward. And when you need to sit back and rest for a while, that's OK too, so don't beat yourself up about it. You may need to reflect and rest for a while but you will never go back.

As you build your strong EBC foundations, and start to wake up to new possibilities, you will notice when you are in flow and out of flow. People and external circumstances will also play a part in how you are feeling so, while it's important to realise that change comes from the inside, it's also important to be aware of the pitfalls as you move forwards.

Our external circumstances sometimes reflect our thinking and thoughts so being around negative people when you're trying to be positive might prove hard work. Transformation is all about making choices, which is why it is so important to find out what you love doing, who you want to be around and who you can't be around. While you are building up your strong foundations, take care to associate with people that will support your path.

It's just a habit

Some people think that being positive and self-discovery work is hard so they don't want to do it every day. However, it is just a habit. You are now aware of your thoughts and how you feel about yourself. By doing more of it, and flexing your mental muscles, the more it will become a habit. Repeatedly telling yourself 'I am amazing' sends new messages to your brain and will help transform any limiting beliefs that may have held you back in the past.

If you have followed the exercises in this book, you will now be in the habit of journaling. I love to journal because it allows me to thrash things out on the page. It's OK to let my negative thoughts and emotions have a voice just for a minute, as I am not giving them any power. I feel able to express myself in my journal and no one can see. All my ideas, dreams and desires and, in fact, the basis of this book were all written in my journal first, so allow the ideas to grow and become a reality if they are right.

So, looking back through your journal, what have you learnt about yourself on this journey?

Sometimes it's difficult to remember where we were and how far we have come. As soon as the pain has gone, we quickly forget the steps we took to help ourselves heal. Whether you have taken a single step or a hundred it is a great achievement. At least you are going forwards rather than feeling lost and stuck. Feel good about the changes you've made. Remember you haven't always been here.

Always remember the journey you have been on.

Moving forwards, continue to trust that you are in control of your life: you can decide how you live it. Trust your decisions and the way you feel and how you can express yourself. No one else knows YOU as well as you do. You have made these changes in your life – so now trust that you know what works for you.

Finally, on a scale of 1–10, with 10 being amazing and 1 being not all, how are you feeling?

Affirmation

'I am courageous and loving my life.'

Conclusion

The Truth

I hope you have experienced plenty of 'aha' moments while reading this book and may have realised that you are not, in fact, lost. All you needed was the right information to help you know the right step to take in order to grow. Feeling lost can be painful, frightening or worrying, but it is also a great thing because it forces us to wake up, to face anything we were previously running from, to act differently and make different choices.

My deepest hope is that by going on this journey with me, you now understand and love yourself more. You may find that the work you've done to build your strong foundations has helped you to transform your life. You may finally get your dream job because you finally know what that is, enjoy more loving relationships with others due to loving yourself, feel more confident about pursuing opportunities when they arise or, most importantly, start living the life you want. Now that's an amazing achievement because the real truth is,

You are amazing.

When I work with clients, I see an amazing person, their amazing soul and the qualities that I have talked about in this book. They are not their problems, they are not depressed or anxious – they are, in fact, just a little lost! The real truth is that you are amazing, you have always been amazing and will continue to be amazing, and it is my job to help you come to the same realisation! But if you still have doubts, then this last exercise is my special gift to you.

Visualisation 5. Meeting the real you

Find somewhere to lie down or sit comfortably where you won't be disturbed.

This is time for YOU, to feel relaxed and at peace.

Take a few deep breaths and let your body and mind relax. Keep following your breath and allow yourself to relax deeply.

Breathe in and out, releasing all negative energy on the breath out.

Breathe in and out.

In your mind's eye, imagine yourself standing on top of a beautiful hill, covered in emerald-green grass. It is a beautiful place and you feel safe.

As you take in the beauty of your surroundings, you notice someone coming towards you in the distance.

You continue to watch this person, curious to see who they are.

You feel a little scared and apprehensive but also feel excited about meeting them.

As this person approaches you, you feel that you know them.

This person is familiar to you but you don't know why. You notice how this person walks, how they are dressed. This person has a confident walk and an inner strength.

This person is happy, confident and successful. You observe how they walk, how they hold themselves.

You love it and you have a sense that you would like to become this person. You feel excited, you feel the possibility that you could be just like them.

You still have the sense that you know who this person is, they feel very familiar to you and you continue to stare and wait.

You love the sparkly energy they are exuding and that attracts you further. It makes you more excited to meet them.

You want more of this person, YOU want to feel this way.

This person continues to approach you and finally you realize why this person seems familiar - it is YOU. The empowered you. The confident you. The YOU that you have been longing for. The lost YOU.

You step towards this person and, as you do they hold out their hand and you take it.

You feel familiar and safe with this person. This person says, 'I knew you were here all along,' "Where have you been?

You reply, 'I thought I would never find you,'

Be willing to accept this is YOU. It was all inside YOU all this time. You just needed to un-reveal your true amazingness. You are this person.

You are happy. You are confident. You are successful. You are amazing.

You embrace this person safe in the knowledge that you are this person and this person is you. As you embrace each other you become one.

Take a few moments to bask in the glory of the empowered you. To feel happy, confident and successful. Enjoy this moment and remember how this feels.

Take a deep breath in and out.

When you are ready wriggle your toes and fingers and open your eyes.

Until next time – be YOU!

Affirmation

'I am amazing.'

About the Author

Ann Hobbs has been training and working to help people discover change for the past 15 years. Her aim is always to help people regain control of their lives. Ann has trained in massage, reflexology, aromatherapy and kinesiology, and brings all of her experiences together in *Kick Ass Your Life*.

Over the last 10 years, Ann has built up a successful practice in Bristol as a holistic therapist, but now also works as a life and business coach with clients all over the country via Skype and phone, using her tried-and-tested techniques to help people kick ass their lives.

Ann has developed a bespoke Kick Ass toolkit of techniques that has helped hundreds of people to create wellbeing and longer-lasting change. Ann loves to inspire others with her speaking events and also offers 'Kick Ass Your Life' workshops. For more information about her workshops and speaking events visit her website. www.annhobbs.co.uk